World War II
Almanac

World War II
Almanac VOLUME 1

George Feldman
Edited by Christine Slovey

AN IMPRINT OF THE GALE GROUP

DETROIT · SAN FRANCISCO · LONDON
BOSTON · WOODBRIDGE, CT

World War II: Almanac

George Feldman

Staff

Christine Slovey, *U•X•L Editor*
Carol DeKane Nagel, *U•X•L Managing Editor*
Tom Romig, *U•X•L Publisher*

Rita Wimberley, *Senior Buyer*
Dorothy Maki, *Manufacturing Manager*
Evi Seoud, *Assistant Production Manager*
Mary Beth Trimper, *Production Director*

Margaret A. Chamberlain, *Permissions Specialist*

Eric Johnson and Martha Schiebold, *Cover Art Directors*
Pamela A. E. Galbreath, *Page Art Director*
Cynthia Baldwin, *Product Design Manager*
Barbara J. Yarrow, *Graphic Services Supervisor*

Linda Mahoney, LM Design, *Typesetting*

Laura Exner, XNR Productions, Inc., *Cartographer*

Front cover photographs reproduced by permission of the National Archives and Records Administration.

Library of Congress Cataloging-in-Publication Data

World War II: Almanac / George Feldman

    cm.

    Includes bibliographical references and index.

    ISBN 0-7876-3830-7 (set), — ISBN 0-7876-3831-5 (v. 1). — ISBN 0-7876-3832-3 (v. 2)

    1. World War, 1939-1945 Juvenile literature.   I. Feldman, George II. Title: World War two. III. Title: World War 2.

D743. 7.W673 1999

940.53—dc21

99-36179
CIP

Printed in the United States of America

10 9 8 7 6 5 4 3 2

Contents

Three children sit in front of their bombed house in London. *(Reproduced by permission of the National Archives and Records Administration)*

Volume 1

U.S. Army tank in Aachen, Germany. *(Reproduced by permission of AP/Wide World Photos)*

Advisory Board

Special thanks are due to U•X•L's World War II Reference Library advisors for their invaluable comments and suggestions:

- Sidney Bolkosky, Professor of History, University of Michigan-Dearborn, Dearborn, Michigan

- Sara Brooke, Director of Libraries, The Ellis School, Pittsburgh, Pennsylvania

- Jacquelyn Divers, Librarian, Roanoke County Schools, Roanoke, Virginia

- Elaine Ezell, Library Media Specialist, Bowling Green Junior High School, Bowling Green, Ohio

- Melvin Small, Department of History, Wayne State University, Detroit, Michigan

Reader's Guide

Between 1939 and 1945 a war was fought among all the major powers of the world. By the end of it, more than fifty countries were involved. It was a war in which more people died than had died in any previous war and it changed the political, social, and economic face of the entire world. *World War II: Almanac* provides a comprehensive range of historical information and current commentary on World War II. The set explores how events after World War I (1914–18) led to World War II; the impact of the rise of dictatorial governments in Europe and of militarism in Japan; how world leaders attempted to avoid war; the relationships among the Allied countries and among the Axis countries; major battles and turning points; life on the home fronts and the nature of German occupations in Europe; scientific developments; art and entertainment during the war; and finally, how the world was changed by the war.

Other Features

World War II: Almanac is divided into seventeen subject chapters, each focusing on a particular topic, such as The Beginning of the War in Europe, Europe Under Occupation,

The War Against Japan, and Spies and Scientists. The chapters contain numerous sidebar boxes, some focusing on people associated with the war, others taking a closer look at pivotal events. More than 150 black-and-white photos and maps illustrate the text. Each volume begins with a timeline of events, a "Words to Know" section, and a "Research and Activity Ideas" section. The volumes conclude with a list of sources students can go to for more information and a subject index so students can easily find the people, places, and events discussed throughout *World War II: Almanac*.

Comments and Suggestions

We welcome your comments on *World War II: Almanac* and suggestions for other topics in history to consider. Please write: Editors, *World War II: Almanac*, U•X•L, 27500 Drake Rd., Farmington Hills, Michigan 48331-3535; call toll-free: 1-800-877-4253; fax to (248)414-5043; or send e-mail via http://www.galegroup.com.

Timeline

1917: The czar (emperor) is overthrown in Russia and a Communist government comes to power. The Russian empire is eventually renamed the Union of Soviet Socialist Republics (USSR), known as the Soviet Union.

1919: Germany signs the Treaty of Versailles, officially ending World War I. Extreme nationalist groups in Germany blame socialists, communists, and Jews for Germany's defeat.

1919: Communist revolutions in various parts of Germany are put down with great bloodshed.

1919: Adolf Hitler joins the tiny German Workers' Party in Munich. The party soon changes its name to the National Socialist German Workers' Party (NSDAP), called the Nazi Party for short.

1908
The Model T Ford
is introduced

1914
World War I
begins

1918
World War I
ends

1920
The League
of Nations
is formed

1905   1910   1915   1920

Unemployed workers turn to a German soup kitchen for a free meal. *(Reproduced by permission of Bildarchiv Preussischer Kulturbesitz)*

1922: Benito Mussolini and his Fascist Party march on Rome, Mussolini is named premier of Italy.

1923: Hyperinflation hits Germany; its currency becomes worthless, causing severe economic distress.

1923: In November, Adolf Hitler leads a failed attempt to take over the German government. Police end the rebellion, called the Munich Beer Hall Putsch, and arrest Hitler and other leaders of the party.

1924: At his trial for treason and armed rebellion, Adolf Hitler gains the attention of extreme nationalists. While serving only eight months of a five year prison sentence, Hitler dictates *Mein Kampf* (*My Struggle*).

1924: Benito Mussolini becomes dictator of Italy.

1926: Hirohito becomes emperor of Japan, giving his reign the name Showa ("enlightened peace").

1927: Chiang Kai-Shek establishes the Kuomintang or Nationalist government in Nanking, China.

1930: A worldwide economic depression hits Germany especially hard. Thirty-three percent of the workforce is unemployed.

1931: The Japanese army seizes Manchuria in a short war with China, establishing Manchuria as the independent country of Manchukuo, which is actually controlled by the Japanese.

1932: In German parliamentary elections held in July, the Nazis become the largest party in Germany, with about 37 percent of the vote. Nazi stormtrooper violence increases.

1932: Franklin D. Roosevelt begins the first of four terms as president of the United States.

1933: Adolf Hitler becomes chancellor (head of the government) of Germany on January 30. Within a few

1922
Harlem Renaissance begins

1924
Vladimir Lenin dies

1926
Germany joins the League of Nations

1929
Great Depression begins; it ends in 1939

1922　　　　　1924　　　　　1926　　　　　1928

months he and his National Socialist German Workers' Party take control of the German government.

1933: The Reichstag building is set afire. Nazis blame the Communists and Hitler receives emergency powers from President Paul von Hindenburg. Free speech and press are restricted. Nazi stormtroopers receive police powers.

1933: Dachau, the first permanent concentration camp, is opened in a suburb of Munich in March. Ten thousand opponents of Nazis, especially communists, are arrested and sent to the newly established concentration camps.

1933: In April, Nazis organize a national boycott of Jewish-owned businesses. The first anti-Jewish laws are passed, removing almost all Jews from government jobs including teaching.

1934: Upon the death of German president Paul von Hindenburg, the office of chancellor is combined with president. Adolf Hitler is now the Führer (leader) of the Third Reich (empire) with absolute powers. All officers and soldiers of the army swear allegiance to Hitler.

1935: March 16, Germany announces the reintroduction of the military draft and a major expansion of its army, violating the Treaty of Versailles.

1935: Germany passes the Nuremberg laws, which define Jews in racial terms, strip them of German citizenship, and ban marriages between Jews and non-Jews.

1935: Italy invades Ethiopia on October 3. By May 1936, Ethiopia is conquered.

1936: Germany and Italy enter into agreements that establish a political and military alliance between the two countries called the "Rome-Berlin Axis."

1936: Germany and Japan sign the Anti-Comintern (anti-communist) Treaty.

German soldiers examining the remains of the burned Reichstag. *(Reproduced by permission of Bildarchiv Preussischer Kulturbesitz)*

1930
The planet Pluto is discovered

1931
The *Star Spangled Banner* is made the national anthem of the United States

1933
Francis Perkins is appointed Secretary of Labor, becoming the first woman to hold a U.S. cabinet post.

1936
The Spanish Civil War begins

1930   1932   1934   1936

Adolf Hitler in Austria.
(Reproduced by permission of AP/Wide World Photos)

1937: In the first example of aerial bombing against a civilian population, the German air force bombs Guernica, Spain, on April 26, aiding Francisco Franco's fascist troops during the Spanish Civil War.

1937: Japan invades China, captures Peking (Beijing), Shanghai, Canton, and other major cities. In Nanking, invading Japanese troops rape, torture, and murder tens of thousands of Chinese civilians.

1938: Austrians vote in favor of the *Anschloss,* an agreement that makes their country part of Nazi Germany. Crowds cheer the German dictator Adolf Hitler as he enters the Austrian capital Vienna.

1938: Soviet and Japanese troops engage in bloody battles on the border of China and Soviet east Asia.

1938: Europe is at the brink of war as Adolf Hitler makes territorial demands on Czechoslovakia. At a conference in Munich in September, leaders of France and Britain agree to grant Germany a section of Czechoslovakia with a large German-speaking population.

1938: November 9, the Nazis stage *Kristallnacht* (Crystal Night or "night of broken glass"), in which homes, businesses, and synagogues of German Jews are destroyed.

1939: Adolf Hitler violates the Munich agreement by taking over the remainder of Czechoslovakia by March 1939.

1939: August 23, Germany and the Soviet Union sign the Nazi-Soviet Pact. The two countries promise not to attack each other and secretly agree to divide Poland after Germany conquers it.

1939: World War II officially begins. Germany invades Poland on September 1; Britain and France declare war on Germany two days later. Poland surrenders on September 27.

1936
The Olympic Games are held in Berlin, Germany

1937
Joseph Stalin conducts purges of the Soviet military and the Communist Party

1938
The first nuclear fission of uranium is produced

1937

1938

1939: Britain begins evacuating children from London to rural towns to protect them from German air raids.

1939: Jews in German-occupied Poland are ordered to wear a yellow star at all times.

1940: April 10, Germany invades Norway and Denmark. Denmark soon surrenders, but fighting continues in Norway, aided by British and French forces. The Norwegian government flees to Britain.

1940: Winston Churchill becomes prime minister of Great Britain.

1940: Germany invades the Netherlands, Belgium, Luxembourg, and France on May 10. The Netherlands surrenders on May 14 and Belgium on May 28.

1940: Italy declares war on France and Britain and invades France on June 10.

1940: French troops evacuate Paris on June 13 and German forces enter the city the next day. France signs an armistice with Germany on June 22. German troops occupy northern France, while a government friendly to Germany (Vichy France) has some independence in the south.

1940: The Germans begin bombing England in a long air campaign called the Battle of Britain. The Germans are defeated by the fighter pilots of Britain's Royal Air Force (RAF) and Hitler abandons plans to invade Britain.

1940: Germany, Japan, and Italy sign a military alliance called the Tripartite Pact. Within six months, Hungary, Romania, Slovakia, and Bulgaria will also join the alliance.

1941: President Franklin D. Roosevelt signs the Lend-Lease Act.

1941: April 13, Japan and the Soviet Union sign a treaty promising that neither will attack the other.

The Polish Cavalry was no match against Germany's tanks.
(Reproduced by permission of AP/Wide World Photos)

1938
The Volkswagen ("people's car") makes its first appearance

March 1939
The Spanish Civil War ends

April 1939
Television broadcasting is introduced at the World's Fair in New York

1939   1940

The Japanese raid on Pearl Harbor. *(Reproduced by permission of the National Archives and Records Administration)*

1941: June 22, Germany invades the Soviet Union in an offensive called Operation Barbarossa and quickly takes control of much of the country.

1941: Winston Churchill and Franklin D. Roosevelt meet aboard a warship off the coast of Newfoundland and issue the Atlantic Charter, in which they agree to promote peace and democracy around the world.

1941: Kiev, the capital of Ukraine, falls to the German army on September 19. On September 29 and 30, thirty-three thousand Jews are killed at Babi Yar outside Kiev.

1941: Japan bombs the U.S. naval base at Pearl Harbor in Hawaii on December 7. The United States and Britain declare war on Japan. Japan's allies, Germany and Italy, declare war on the United States on December 10.

1942: In January, the U.S. Ration board announces rationing of rubber. In May, sugar is rationed. By the end of the year, gasoline is also being rationed.

1942: Manila, capital of the Philippines, surrenders to the Japanese on January 2.

1942: Executive Order 9066 directs all Japanese Americans living on the West Coast to internment camps.

1942: May 6, American and Filipino troops on the island of Corregidor in Manila Bay surrender to the Japanese.

1942: May 7, the U.S. Navy defeats the Japanese fleet in the Battle of the Coral Sea in the Pacific.

1942: In May, 1,000 British bombers destroy Cologne, Germany's third largest city.

1942: The Americans defeat the Japanese fleet at the Battle of Midway, June 4 to 7, in one of the most decisive naval battles in history.

1942: In July, British bombers attack Germany's second largest city, Hamburg, on four straight nights, causing a firestorm that kills 30,000 civilians.

1940
The Olympic Games Committee cancels the games

1941
Hideki Tojo becomes prime minister of Japan

1942
Oxfam is founded to fight world famine

1941

1942

1942: August 7, American troops land on Guadalcanal in the Solomon Islands in the mid-Pacific, the first American offensive operation of the war.

1942: In the Battle of El Alamein in Egypt, the British Eighth Army wins a strategic victory against Italian forces and the German Afrika Korps.

1942: November 8, the Allies launch Operation Torch, an invasion of German-occupied North Africa that ends with the Germans being chased from the region.

1943: January 31, the Germans surrender to the Russian troops at Stalingrad, marking a major turning point of the war.

1943: Small groups of Jews in the Warsaw ghetto begin attacking German troops on April 19. They continue fighting for almost one month until the Germans have killed almost all of the Jewish resisters and completely destroyed the ghetto.

1943: July 10, American, British, and Canadian troops land on Sicily, a large island south of the Italian mainland, and defeat German forces there.

1943: Italian dictator Benito Mussolini is removed from office by the Fascist Grand Council on July 25 and tries to establish a separate government in northern Italy.

1943: The Allies invade the Italian mainland on September 3; the new Italian government surrenders to the Allies on September 8.

1944: June 6, Allied forces land in Normandy in the largest sea invasion in history, called Operation Overlord.

1944: On the third anniversary of the German invasion of the Soviet Union, June 22, the Soviets launch a massive offensive called Operation Bagration, inflicting immense losses on the German army and driving them back almost 400 miles in a month.

American and Filipino troops surrender at Corregidor. *(Reproduced by permission of the Corbis Corporation [Bellevue])*

1942
Physicist Enrico Fermi achieves the first sustained nuclear chain reaction

1943
Prohibition of Chinese immigration into the United States is repealed

October 1943
Chicago's first subway is dedicated

1943   1944

Survivors of the Warsaw Ghetto uprising are rounded up at gunpoint. *(Reproduced by permission of AP/Wide World Photos)*

1944: July 20, a group of German army officers attempt to kill German leader Adolf Hitler and make peace with the Allies. Many of the conspirators, along with their families, are tortured and executed in retaliation.

1944: August 25, Paris is liberated by Free French and American forces.

1944: The largest naval battle in history, the Battle of Leyte Gulf in the Philippines, October 23 to 26, ends in the almost total destruction of the Japanese fleet.

1944: December 16, the Germans launch a major counter-offensive against the Americans in the Ardennes Forest, known as the Battle of the Bulge.

1945: January 12, the Soviets begin an offensive along the entire Polish front, entering Warsaw on January 17, and Lodz two days later. By February 1, they are within 100 miles of the German capital of Berlin.

1945: January 18, the Nazis begin evacuating the Auschwitz death camp. Almost 60,000 surviving prisoners are forced on a death march out of the camp.

1945: February 14, Allied raids on Dresden result in firestorms while the city is crammed with German refugees from the fighting farther east.

1945: February 19, American Marines land on Iwo Jima in the Pacific.

1945: March 7, American troops cross the Rhine River in Germany, the last natural obstacle between the Allied forces and Berlin.

1945: American troops land on Okinawa on April 1, beginning the largest land battle of the Pacific war. The Japanese forces are defeated by June.

1945: April 12, U.S. president Franklin D. Roosevelt dies; Harry S. Truman becomes president of the United States.

1946
Cold War begins

1947
India gains independence from Great Britain

1948
Israel is declared an independent state

1945   1946   1947   1948

1945: April 28, former Italian dictator Benito Mussolini is captured by resistance fighters and executed.

1945: With Soviet troops in the city limits, Adolf Hitler commits suicide in his fortified bunker beneath Berlin on April 30. The new German government surrenders unconditionally on May 8.

1945: July 16, the first atomic bomb is tested in the desert near Alamogordo, New Mexico.

1945: August 6, the United States drops an atomic bomb on Hiroshima, Japan. A second bomb is dropped on Nagasaki, Japan, on August 9.

1945: August 8, the Soviet Union declares war on Japan; a large Soviet force invades Manchuria the following day.

1945: August 15, the Allies accept the unconditional surrender of Japan. Formal surrender papers are signed aboard the USS *Missouri* in Tokyo Bay on September 2.

1945: War crimes trials begin in Nuremberg, Germany, in November.

1948: The Soviets block all overland traffic between Berlin and the Allied-controlled zones of Germany. Allies airlift food and fuel to West Berlin for eleven months.

1949: The Soviets establish East Germany as a Communist state called the German Democratic Republic; France, England, and the United States join their power zones into a democratic state called the Federal Republic of Germany (West Germany).

1949: Communists led by Mao Zedong take control of China; Chiang Kai-shek and the Nationalists are forced into exile on Taiwan.

1952: General Dwight D. Eisenhower becomes president of the United States.

1961: Communists build the Berlin Wall around East Berlin

1949
The North Atlantic Treaty Organization (NATO) is created

1950
The Korean War begins; it ends in 1953

1951
J. D. Salinger's *Catcher in the Rye* is published

1949   1950   1951   1952

in order to stop East Germans seeking a higher standard of living from fleeing to West Germany through West Berlin.

1988: The U.S. Congress formally apologizes to Japanese Americans for interning them in concentration camps during World War II. Living persons who spent time in the camps are offered a one-time payment of $20,000.

1989: The Berlin Wall is destroyed.

1990: East Germany and West Germany are reunited.

1998: Volkswagen agrees to pay reparations to slave laborers who worked in their factories during the war.

1999: Dinko Sakic, the last known living commander of a World War II concentration camp, is tried for war crimes.

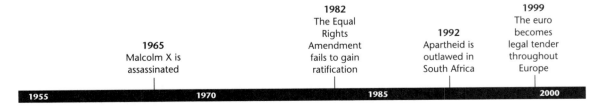

1982
The Equal
Rights
Amendment
fails to gain
ratification

1965
Malcolm X is
assassinated

1992
Apartheid is
outlawed in
South Africa

1999
The euro
becomes
legal tender
throughout
Europe

1955   1970   1985   2000

Words to Know

A

Afrika Korps: The experienced, effective German troops who fought under German field marshal Erwin Rommel in the North African desert.

Allies: The countries who fought against Germany, Italy, and Japan during World War II. The makeup of the Allied powers changed over the course of the war. The first major Allied countries were Great Britain and France. Germany defeated France in 1940 but some Free French forces continued to fight with the Allies until the end of the war. The Soviet Union and the United States joined the Allies in 1941.

Annex: To add territory to an existing country.

Anschloss: The 1938 agreement that made Austria a part of Nazi Germany.

Anti-Comintern Treaty: Comintern refers to the Communist International organization, a group of world Communist parties that was run by the Soviet Union. Germany, Japan, and Italy called their military alliance

Anti-Comintern to make it sound like a defensive agreement against communism.

Anti-Semitism: The hatred of Jews, who are sometimes called Semites.

Appeasement: Making compromises in order to stay on neutral terms with another party or country.

Armistice: A temporary halt to a war, until a peace treaty ends it permanently.

Armored division: A division of the army that uses tanks.

Atlantic Charter: An agreement signed in 1941 by President Franklin D. Roosevelt and British prime minister Winston Churchill in which the United States and Great Britain stated their commitment to worldwide peace and democracy.

Atom bomb: A weapon of mass destruction in which a radioactive element such as uranium is bombarded with neutrons to create a chain reaction called nuclear fission, releasing a huge amount of energy.

Axis: During World War II, Germany, Italy, and Japan formed a coalition called the Axis powers. Eventually, they were joined by Hungary, Romania, Slovakia, Finland, and Bulgaria.

B

Black market: Where rationed goods are bought and sold illegally, in violation of government restrictions.

Blitzkrieg: Meaning "lightning war" in German, this is the name given the German's military strategy of sending troops in land vehicles to make quick, surprise attacks while airplanes provide support from above. This strategy was especially effective against Poland and France.

C

Calvary: Originally referred to horse-mounted troops. In modern times calvary refers to troops using armored vehicles such as tanks.

Chancellor: In some European countries, including Germany, the chief minister of the government.

Collaborate: To work together toward a common goal; during wartime this term refers to working with the enemy force that has occupied one's country.

Communism: An economic system that promotes the ownership of most property and means of production by the community as a whole. By 1939, the Soviet Union was a harsh dictatorship run by the Communist Party and its all-powerful leader, Josef Stalin.

Concentration camps: Places where the Germans confined people they considered enemies of the state. These included Jews, Roma (commonly called Gypsies), homosexuals, and political opponents.

Convoys: Large groups traveling together, sometimes with military protection, for safety.

D

D-Day: Usually refers to June 6, 1944, the day the Normandy Invasion began with a massive landing of Allied troops on the beaches of northern France, which was occupied by Germany; also called Operation Overlord. D-Day is also a military term designating the date and time of an attack.

Death camps: Concentration camps built by the Nazis for the single purpose of killing Jews.

Depression: An economic downturn with falling industrial production, lower prices, and increasing unemployment. The United States experienced the worst depression in its history from 1929 to 1939, which is referred to as the Great Depression.

Dictator: A ruler who holds absolute power.

Division: A large unit of an army, usually about 15,000 men.

Draft: The system by which able young men are required by law to perform a term of military service for their country.

E

Einsatzgruppen: Meaning "special-action groups" in German, these were specially trained strike forces in the military wing of the Nazi Party that were responsible for murdering approximately 2 million Jews, Communists, and other people in the Soviet Union.

Embargo: A government ban on trade.

Executive Order 9066: President Franklin D. Roosevelt's order directing all Japanese Americans living on the American West Coast to be sent to internment camps.

Exile: Living away from one's native country, either by choice or by force.

Extermination camps: Concentration camps built by the Nazis with the single purpose of killing Jews.

F

Fascism: A political system in which power rests not with citizens but with the central government, which is often run by the military and/or a dictator.

Final Solution: The code name given to the Nazi plan to eliminate all the Jews of Europe.

Free French Movement: The movement led by Charles de Gaulle, who,, from a position outside France, tried to organize and encourage the French people to resist the German occupation.

Führer: The German word meaning "leader"; the title Adolf Hitler took as dictator of Germany.

G

G.I.: Standing for government issue, a nickname for enlisted soldiers or former members of the U.S. armed forces.

Genocide: The deliberate, systematic destruction of a racial, national, or cultural group.

Gestapo: An abbreviation for Germany's *Geheime Staats Politzei* or Secret State Police.

Gliders: Planes without motors that are towed by ropes behind regular planes and then cut loose and allowed to float down to land.

Guerillas: People who fight behind enemy lines, usually employing hit-and-run tactics against a more powerful enemy.

H

Hitler Youth: An organization that trained German boys to idolize and obey German leader Adolf Hitler and to become Nazi soldiers.

Holocaust: The period between 1933 and 1945 when Nazi Germany systematically persecuted and murdered millions of Jews, Roma (commonly called Gypsies), homosexuals, and other innocent people.

I

Internment camps: A guarded facility usually used to hold citizens of an enemy country during wartime. The United States had ten camps located throughout the western part of the country to which about 120,000 Americans of Japanese ancestry were forced to move due to the ungrounded suspicion that they were not loyal to the United States.

Isolationism: A country's policy of keeping out of other countries' affairs. Isolationism was a strong force in American politics after World War I (1914–18) and continued to be an important factor until Japan attacked the United States in December 1941.

L

Lebensraum: A German term meaning "room to live." The Nazis told the German people that they needed expanded living space to survive and used this idea as justification for invading and occupying other countries.

Lend-Lease Program: A program that allowed the United States to send countries fighting the Germans (such as

Great Britain and the Soviet Union) supplies needed for the war effort in exchange for payment to be made after the war.

Luftwaffe: The German air force.

M

Manhattan Project: The project funded by the U.S. government that gathered scientists together at facilities in Chicago, Illinois, Los Alamos, New Mexico, and other places to work on the development of an atom bomb.

Martial law: Temporary rule of the government by the military, often imposed during war or other emergencies. Under martial law, many normal legal rights are suspended.

***Mein Kampf* (*My Struggle*):** The 1924 autobiography of Adolf Hitler, in which he explains his racial and political philosophies, including his hatred of Jews.

Merchant ships: Commercial or trading ships.

Militarists: Extremists in the military and their supporters who believe the government should be controlled by the army and society should be organized on military principles.

Mobilized: Called to active duty in the armed services.

Morale: The state of a person's or group's spirit and willingness to work toward an established goal.

N

Nationalism: Strong loyalty to one's nation, combined with a belief that one's country will benefit from acting independently and in its own best interest rather than in cooperation with other countries. Nationalism often leads to dislike of other countries.

Nazi: The abbreviated name for the National Socialist German Workers' Party, the political party led by Adolf Hitler, who became dictator of Germany. Hitler's Nazi Party controlled Germany from 1933 to 1945. The

Nazis promoted racist and anti-Semitic (anti-Jewish) ideas and enforced complete obedience to Hitler and the party.

Noncombatant: A job in the military that is not directly involved with combat or fighting.

O

Occupation: Control of a country by a foreign military power.

Operation Overlord: The code name for the Normandy Invasion, a massive Allied attack on German-occupied France; also called D-Day.

P

Partisans: Groups fighting behind enemy lines or in occupied territory, usually employing hit-and-run tactics.

Pearl Harbor: Inlet on the southern coast of the island of Oahu, Hawaii, and the site of a Japanese attack on a U.S. naval base on December 7, 1941. The attack prompted the United States to enter World War II.

Prime minister: Chief executive of the government or of parliament.

Propaganda: Material such as literature, images, or speeches that is designed to influence public opinion toward a certain doctrine. The content of the material may be true or false and is often political.

Purge: To remove (often by killing) all those who are seen as enemies.

R

Ration: To make something available in fixed amounts; limiting access to scarce goods; the allotted amount of something.

Red Army: Another name for the Soviet Union's army.

Refugee: A person escaping from danger or persecution.

Reich: The German word meaning "empire"; Adolf Hitler's term as Germany's leader was called the Third Reich.

Reichstag: Germany's parliament or lawmaking body.

Reparations: Compensation required from a defeated nation for damage or injury during war.

Resistance: Working against an occupying army.

S

SA: An abbreviation for *Sturmabteilungen,* or stormtroopers. They were members of a special armed and uniformed branch of the Nazi Party.

Sabotage: Intentional destruction of military or industrial facilities.

Segregation: The forced separation of black and white people, not only in public places and schools but also in the U.S. military. The opposite of segregation is integration.

Socialism: A political system in which the means of producing and distributing goods are shared or owned by the government.

Soviet Union: Short for the Union of Soviet Socialist Republics or USSR, the country that the Communists had set up after overthrowing the Russian Empire.

SS: An abbreviation for *Schutzstaffel,* or Security Squad, the unit that provided German leader Adolf Hitler's personal bodyguards as well as guards for the various concentration camps.

Stormtroopers: Another name for members of the *Sturmabteilungen,* a special armed and uniformed branch of the Nazi Party.

Swastika: The Nazi symbol of a black, bent-armed cross that always appeared within a white circle set on a red background.

Synagogue: A Jewish house of worship.

T

Theater: An area of operations during a war. The main areas of operation during World War II were the European theater and the Pacific theater.

Tripartite Pact: An agreement signed in September 1940 that established an alliance among Germany, Italy, and Japan. The countries promised to aid each other should any one of them face an attack.

U

U-boat: Nickname given to German submarines because the German word for submarine is *unterseeboots*.

Underground: Engaged in secret or illegal activity.

V

Versailles Treaty: The agreement signed by the countries who had fought in World War I that required Germany to claim responsibility for the war and pay money to other countries for damage from the war.

Veteran: A person who has served in the armed forces.

Vichy Government: The government set up in France after the Germans invaded the country; headed by Henri Petain, it was really under German control.

W

WACs: The Women's Army Corps, an organization that allowed American women to serve in a variety of non-combat roles.

Waffen-SS: Also known as the "armed SS," military units of the SS that fought as part of the regular army.

War crimes: Violations of the laws or customs of war.

Research and Activity Ideas

The following research and activity ideas are intended to offer suggestions for complementing social studies and history curricula, to trigger additional ideas for enhancing learning, and to suggest cross-disciplinary projects for library and classroom use.

Ration Recipes: Look in cookbooks published during the 1940s or in women's magazines published during World War II and note how the recipes account for rationing. Make one of the recipes and invite others to rate the flavor, or adapt a recipe from a modern cookbook to account for rationing.

Personal History: Interview a veteran of World War II or someone who lived during the war. Create a list of questions before the interview. You might find out where your subject was during the war, how the war changed his or her life, his or her impression of the importance of the war both at the time and in the world after the war.

Atom bomb debate: Study the decision to drop atom bombs on Hiroshima and Nagasaki. Taking into consideration only what was known at the time about the bombs, form two teams, one in favor of dropping the bomb and the other against it, and debate the issues. Then, repeat the debate taking into consideration what we know now about the effects of atomic bombs. Discuss how the debate changed.

Turning Points: On a large map of the world use pushpins to mark the sites of battles that were important turning points during the war. For each site create a notecard that explains who fought in the battle, who the was the victor, and why the battle there was important.

Modern opinions from historical figures: Form a group of four to six people. Choose a current event in world politics (such as NATO's actions in Kosovo); prepare for a panel discussion on the topic by reading magazine and newspaper articles and Internet news stories on the subject. Choose one person to serve as a discussion moderator. Everyone else in the group should choose a prominent individual involved in World War II whom he or she will represent in a panel discussion. Each person should research the individual he or she has selected and have a clear understanding of the historical figure's role in the war. The group will then have a panel discussion on the selected current event with students presenting the positions they think their historical figure would take on the subject.

War-inspired artwork: Choose a creative work related to World War II. This can be anything from one of the many War memorials, like the memorial to the USS *Arizona* in Pearl Harbor, Hawaii, to a poem, song, or painting inspired by the war, such as Randall Jarrell's poem "The Death of a Ball Turret Gunner." Explain the work's relationship to the war: is it about a battle, or an individual's experience of the war? What emotions does the piece evoke: bravery, fear, loneliness, anger?

War journal: Imagine that you are a child living during the war. You can choose to have lived in any of the countries involved in the war. Write a journal of your activities over the course of one week.

Propaganda: Rent a video of a film created during the war and one that has a war theme. Some examples of films that are available on videocassette include: Frank Capra's *Why We Fight* series of documentaries, *Casablanca, Mrs. Miniver,* and *Der Führer's Face.* Write an essay discussing whether the film has a particular political message and discuss what that message is.

Battlefield tour: Pretend that you are a travel agent and create a World War II battlefield tour. You could choose to focus the tour on sites in the Pacific, sites throughout Europe or North Africa, or focus on a specific country. List the sites you'll be visiting on the tour, giving the name of the battle, if there was a codename for the operation, key events of the battle and the commanders involved, who won the battle, and why it was important.

D-Day Newspaper article: Imagine you are a war correspondent for either a U.S. paper or a German paper covering the June 6, 1944, invasion of France. Write an article about the events you see.

World War II
Almanac

Background to War

The Second World War was fought from 1939 to 1945. In those six years, more soldiers were killed than in any war that had ever been fought. More civilians died because of the war than ever before in history. In no other war did so many people lose their homes, their possessions, their whole way of life. The total number of deaths from World War II has been estimated at 50 million, which is about 1 out of every 5 people in the United States today.

The most terrible war

World War II was the first time a war was fought all over the world. By the time it ended, there had been fighting on every continent except South America and Antarctica, and in almost all the oceans. Armies had battled one another on jungle islands in the Pacific Ocean, and in the deserts of North Africa. Planes had bombed Australia and Hawaii, London and Moscow, Norway and Egypt. Large parts of Europe and eastern Asia were in ruins. Two cities in Japan, Hiroshima and Nagasaki, had been utterly destroyed by atomic bombs.

Almost 6 million Jews, including 1.5 million children, had been murdered in Europe simply because they were Jews.

Nazi Germany and the special nature of World War II

From 1933 until 1945 Germany was ruled by Adolf Hitler and the National Socialist German Workers' Party (the Nazis). This was a harsh and brutal government. Any opponent of the Nazis was arrested and sent—without a trial—to a concentration camp. Concentration camps were brutal prison camps run by Nazi soldiers. The Nazis controlled what could be published in newspapers and magazines, what was reported on radio broadcasts, and what books people could read. The Nazis' main political goal—to make Germany the ruler of Europe—and their theories about race contributed greatly to the brutality of World War II. Hitler believed that Germany needed *Lebensraum* or "room to live" if it was to survive. The Nazis also believed that Germans were a master race, superior to all others, and that the superior race had a right to attack, conquer, and enslave weaker ones. Based on these beliefs the Nazis justified the murder and enslavement of the citizens of countries it conquered. Eventually, the Nazis instituted an official policy of mass murder that led to the systematic murder of 6 million Jews.

Two theaters of war

This terrible destruction began as two separate wars, one in Europe and one in eastern Asia. The background and causes of these two wars were different. In Asia and the Pacific, the war was fought between Japan and several countries, but mainly with China, Great Britain, and the United States. The background to that war was Japan's attempt to control much of Asia.

Japan invaded Manchuria, a region of China, in 1931. At the time China was in the middle of a civil war (different factions of the government were fighting each other for control of the country), and did not immediately resist this invasion. War finally broke out between Japan and China in 1937, as Japan moved to take over the rest of China. Japan also began expanding its empire to the Pacific islands off the coast of the Asian continent. Much of this territory was controlled by such countries as the United States, Great Britain, and the Netherlands. Japan prepared to go to war with these countries over the territory. In December 1941, Japan bombed the U.S. port of Pearl Harbor on the Hawaiian Islands and America declared war on Japan.

The other war began as a European war. Although almost every nation in Europe was soon involved, a few countries played more prominent roles. It began in September 1939 when Germany launched an attack on Poland and found itself facing Great Britain and France, who had sworn to defend Poland should the Germans attack it. Great Britain, France, and the countries that would eventually join them against Germany were called the Allied powers. Germany was joined by Italy and later by Japan to form the Axis powers.

Although the Allies declared war on Germany in 1939, the fighting didn't begin until the spring of 1940 when Germany invaded Denmark, Norway, France, Belgium, Luxembourg, and the Netherlands. In June 1941, Germany attacked the Soviet Union (Russia). In December 1941, it declared war on the United States. By that time, Germany had conquered much of Europe.

Great Britain, France, and the countries that would eventually join them against Germany were called the Allied powers. Germany was joined by Italy and later by Japan to form the Axis powers.

Memory of another war in Europe

When war came in September 1939, the people of Europe were still haunted by the memory of World War I. Fought from 1914 to 1918, this war began as a conflict between Austria-Hungary and Serbia and escalated into a war involving 32 countries. On one side were Austria-Hungary, Bulgaria, Germany, and Turkey, fighting against 28 other nations, including France, Great Britain, the Soviet Union, and the United States.

To many people, that war now seemed senseless. It hadn't accomplished much, except to destroy a whole generation of young men. In Germany alone, almost 2 million German soldiers had been killed and another 4 million had been wounded. In France and Britain (the major European powers that along with the United States had won World War I), the memory of this slaughter was a very important factor in the years between the two world wars. The idea that there would be another war seemed unthinkable. Some countries felt that almost any price should be paid to avoid that possibility.

Many Germans were also horrified by the memory of World War I. But Germany was on the losing side of the war and its experiences after World War I were different from those of the victorious countries. The events in Germany after World War I led to the rise of the National Socialist German Workers' Party (the Nazis) and put Europe on the road to World War II.

The end of World War I

World War I started in 1914 and after a few years of fighting the armies and people of Europe were exhausted. So many men had been killed, wounded, or taken prisoner that both sides were running out of soldiers. In 1917, the United States joined Britain and France (known as the Allies) in the war against Germany. As hundreds of thousands of fresh American troops began arriving in Europe, it became clear that Germany would run out of men first.

The British fleet prevented all ships, including those carrying food, from reaching German ports, and hunger was increasing. Germany's allies, the Austrian Empire and Turkey, were collapsing. The German generals knew that the war was lost, and they told the German emperor, the kaiser, that Germany had to give up.

Then, a revolution broke out in Germany. In the face of the growing disorder throughout the country, the kaiser left on November 10. The next day, November 11, 1918, the new leaders of the German government signed an armistice with the Allies, ending the Great War. (An armistice is a temporary halt to a war, until a peace treaty ends it permanently.)

The Treaty of Versailles

The new government of Germany had to negotiate a permanent peace treaty with the Allies. The Treaty of Versailles, named after the city near Paris where the Peace Con-

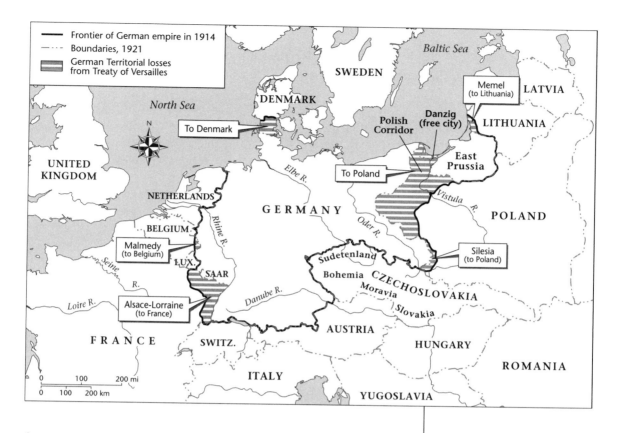

ference met, was intended to make Germany permanently poor and weak. The terms were very harsh. The German armed forces were strictly limited. The army could have only 100,000 men, the navy 15,000. They could have no planes, tanks, or submarines.

Germany lost all its colonies, which were taken over mainly by France and Britain. Germany also lost some of its own territory. Alsace and Lorraine, which Germany had taken from France after a war in 1870, went back to France. A section of western Germany near France, called the Rhineland, would be controlled by Allied troops for a number of years, and no German armed forces would be allowed there. Large sections of eastern Germany went to the newly independent country of Poland. These areas had been in German hands since before 1800, when Poland had been divided among Russia, the Austrian Empire, and Prussia, the country that later became the modern country of Germany. The easternmost part of Germany (called East Prussia) was cut off from the rest of the coun-

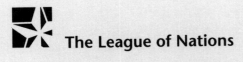

The League of Nations

A result of the Treaty of Versailles was the creation of the League of Nations. This organization of countries was supposed to work together to solve international problems peacefully, much like the United Nations today. The League had some minor successes, such as holding elections in disputed areas to allow the people who lived there to decide what country they wanted to be part of. But the League's real purpose was to prevent war by "collective security." This meant that all the member states would protect each other from being attacked by an enemy. The idea was that members of the League would use their economic power to punish an attacker, or they would even use force to defend a weak country.

But the League of Nations failed completely in these goals. One reason, according to historians, was that the United States refused to join, even though the League was originally the idea of Woodrow Wilson, the president during and after World War I. It was the United States Senate that rejected joining the League, reasoning that it did not want the United States to continue to be mixed up in Europe's problems. Like the Senate, many Americans believed that their men had died in World War I over disputes that had nothing to do with the United States. This feeling, called isolationism, was a strong force in American politics, and it continued to be an important factor until Japan attacked the United States in December 1941.

America's absence from the League made it seem less of a neutral body than it was meant to be. Without U.S. participation, many saw the League as a way for Britain and France to protect their own interests and enforce their own wills on the rest of Europe. Although the League continued to meet and vote on important issues, the world paid less and less attention to its decisions.

try by a section of Poland that became known as the "Polish Corridor." Germany lost about one-eighth of its territory.

War guilt and reparations

The Allies made two other demands that angered Germans more than anything else. They forced Germany to admit that it was responsible for starting the war. The Allies demanded that Germany make payments to them, especially to France, for the enormous destruction the war caused. When the amount of these reparations (repayments) was later revealed, it was staggering. According to the Allied demands, Germany would continue making reparations for almost sixty more years.

No one in Germany liked the treaty, especially the admission of guilt for starting the war. But the threat of the Allied armies invading the country meant that Germany had no choice, and it signed the treaty.

The "stab in the back"

Because of the way the war ended, with the confusion of revolution and the kaiser who had started the war leaving his country without resolving it, an important myth developed. Some Germans said that their armies had never been defeated. They believed that Germany had lost the war because the army had been "stabbed in the back" by the leaders who surrendered. This idea was most popular among extreme nationalists, people with intense feelings of loyalty to their nation who combined these emotions with a dislike of other countries and foreigners.

They accused the new democratic government that replaced the kaiser of betraying Germany. They also blamed Jews, socialists, and communists. Socialism is a political and economic system based on government control of the production and distribution of goods. The German socialist party, called the Social Democrats, was very large, and became the most important party in the new German government. Communism is similar to socialism; communists believe that the community as a whole should share ownership of the methods of production of the country (the factories and farms for example) and share equally the goods (food and all other products) produced by the country. Unlike the socialists in Germany, who argued for changing the government slowly, the communists wanted an immediate revolution.

The myths that these groups had betrayed Germany in World War II by surrendering helped prepare the way for a leader who promised to make Germany strong again and who promised to punish the "traitors" who had "stabbed Germany in the back."

In July 1919, it took about 14 marks to buy 1 American dollar. By mid-November 1923, 1 American dollar was worth 2.52 trillion German marks.

During the next several years, different groups—including the communists and extreme nationalists—made repeated attempts to overthrow the new government. The government defeated each of these attempts, but at a high cost. Often, the government depended on extreme nationalist volunteer troops to defeat the communists. There were brutal street battles that sometimes approached civil war.

Economic disasters

The German economy was badly weakened by the war, by the disorder that continued around the country, and by war reparations. Economic disaster struck in the early 1920s in the form of hyperinflation, an extremely fast increase in prices. In July 1919, it took about 14 marks (the German unit of money) to buy 1 American dollar. By July 1922, it took about 490. A year later, 1 dollar was worth almost 3 million marks. By mid-November 1923, 1 American dollar was worth 2.52 trillion German marks.

The value of pensions and bank accounts was wiped out. Savings that once would have bought a house now would not pay for a loaf of bread. Most middle class people fell from comfort to poverty. Many Germans became fearful about the future and distrusted the government. When a new economic disaster struck Germany at the beginning of the 1930s, many of them had no faith in the political parties that were loyal to the new German government. They supported the newly founded Nazi party instead.

The Great Depression

For a short while, in the mid- to late 1920s, Germany became more prosperous. The inflation was brought under control, and German industry was producing as many products as it had before World War I. Then in the fall of 1929, an economic crisis called a depression hit the United States. A depression is a period of falling industrial production, lower prices, and increasing unemployment. Depressions had occurred periodically, but this one was much more severe and would come to be called the Great Depression. Companies could not sell

their products, so they had to let many of their employees go, or even closed their factories. Fewer people had jobs, so they could not afford to buy anything. That meant that companies sold even fewer products, and closed even more factories.

Although it began in the United States, the crisis soon spread to all the industrial countries of Europe. The economies of all these countries were connected. They bought and sold each other's products. The United States had been the strongest and largest economy in the world. Now, it was very difficult to sell anything in the United States.

The depression in Germany

Germany was hit harder by the depression than any other major European country. Partly this was because German companies depended more than others on exporting their products to other countries. During the good economic

Many unemployed workers had to turn to soup kitchens for free meals during Germany's depression.
(Reproduced by permission of Bildarchiv Preussischer Kulturbesitz)

times of the late 1920s, one-third of German products were exported. The countries Germany exported to were also affected by the depression and couldn't buy as many of its products.

German banks closed, and industrial production fell rapidly. Unemployment was the worst problem. By early 1933, 6 million Germans were unemployed and only about 12 million still had jobs: 1 out of 3 Germans was out of work. The unemployed and their families were becoming desperate as the government seemed unable—or unwilling—to solve the problem.

Nazis popularity grows

As unemployment grew, so did a willingness to turn to political parties who were completely against the system. The National Socialist German Workers' Party (the Nazis), who had been a party on the fringe of German politics, suddenly became a major force.

Their leader, Adolf Hitler, told his audiences that he would make Germany strong and prosperous again, though he did not explain how. Instead, he stirred up hatred. He had one explanation for every problem people faced and one enemy for them to focus on: Jews. His hatred of the Jews was both his deepest belief and a tactic to win people over to his side. Many of the middle-class people who listened to him thought that Hitler and the Nazis were Germany's last hope.

While Hitler made his speeches, the Nazis also used street violence to frighten their opponents, break up their political meetings, and beat up Jews on the street. A giant army of uniformed Nazi thugs, called stormtroopers, became more and more powerful. In 1931, there were 170,000 stormtroopers, and a year later over 400,000. At the time, the official Germany army was limited to 100,000 men.

Stormtrooper violence was not just a sidelight for the Nazis. They glorified violence as an expression of strength. The Nazis were often referred to as "fascists." Fascism is a political movement marked by extreme nationalism, celebration of military strength, strong anticommunism, and a belief in a single all-powerful leader. Fascists do not pretend to be democratic,

like other dictators often do. Instead, they openly express contempt for democracy, which they describe as weak and old, in contrast to fascism, which is supposed to be young, healthy, and strong. Using military-style organizations, like the stormtroopers, to help them gain power is one of the most common features of fascist movements. Once in power, fascist governments continue using violence to repress all political opponents and independent organizations, such as labor unions.

Nazi stormtroopers in 1923. The stormtroopers used violence to silence opponents and to intimidate others to join the Nazi Party. *(Reproduced by permission of Bildarchiv Preussischer Kulturbesitz)*

Political deadlock

The political parties that supported the government could not agree on how to deal with the depression. The conservative parties, supported by big business and many middle-class people, wanted to cut benefits to the unemployed, cut the pay of government employees, and raise taxes on people who still had jobs. But the Social Democrats, the moderate socialist party that was the largest in Germany,

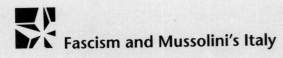

Fascism and Mussolini's Italy

The name "fascist" came from Italy. It was the political party of the Italian dictator, Benito Mussolini. In many ways, German leader Adolf Hitler followed the example of the Italian fascists. Nazi stormtroopers, often called brownshirts, were modeled after Mussolini's "black shirts," the gangs of fascist thugs who beat up his opponents.

Just as in Germany, the years immediately after World War I were a period of turmoil in Italy. Even though Italy, unlike Germany, was on the winning side in World War I, it felt that it had not gotten the territory—or the respect—that it deserved in the peace settlement. Italy was much poorer than Britain, France, or Germany, and the disruption of the war brought out the dissatisfaction of the Italian people. A wave of strikes and factory take-overs by workers swept the country.

Mussolini and his Fascist Party promised a return to order and discipline, as well as glory and prosperity for Italy. Much as happened in Germany with the Nazis a decade later, many powerful forces in Italy decided that the Fascists were their best hope to maintain their own power. They made Mussolini head of the government in 1922.

Mussolini established the Fascists as the only legal party, destroying all

wanted to continue high unemployment benefits and raise taxes on the rich.

Neither side could get a majority of votes in the Reichstag (the German national legislature, equivalent to Congress in the United States) so the legislature remained deadlocked. The conservative chancellor (the head of the government, and also called the prime minister) called new elections for September 1930. He hoped that the voters would elect enough people who agreed with him to break the deadlock.

The Nazis stun Germany

The results of the election stunned everyone. The Nazis received almost 6.5 million votes, and won 107 seats in the Reichstag. Two years earlier, they had gotten 809,000 votes and 12 seats. They were now the second largest party in Ger-

opposition by force. He built huge buildings as part of his promise to make Italy glorious, as in the days of the ancient Roman Empire. He built up the armed forces. Then in 1935, Italy invaded Ethiopia, one of the only countries in Africa that was not a colony of one of the European nations. This was supposed to be the beginning of Italy's return to glory.

After Hitler and the Nazis took over Germany, Italy and Germany became close allies. Apart from their similar outlooks, the two governments shared some common goals. Both countries were interested in change, while Britain and France wanted to maintain the existing situation. For example, Italy's desire for an African empire challenged British and French control of their colonies. Both Italy and Germany wanted governments friendly to them in Europe. To help meet this goal, Italy sent troops to help General Francisco Franco's pro-fascist rebels in the Spanish Civil War that began in 1936, while Germany sent airmen and planes. Soon, however, it became clear that Germany, with its much greater economic and military power, was the senior partner and that Hitler—not Mussolini—was the leader of the fascist movement in Europe.

many. The new Reichstag was even less able to agree on anything than before the elections. The conservatives could not form a majority by themselves without including the Nazis.

This deadlock continued for months. During that time, the president of Germany, Paul von Hindenburg, had to run for re-election. (Hindenburg was a national hero who had commanded the German army in World War I but was now 85 years old. As president he was head of state, largely a symbolic position, though he did carry considerable influence in government.) In a four-way race, Hitler received over 11 million votes, about 30 percent of the total. In the run-off election, he received almost 13.5 million votes, almost 37 percent. Although Hindenburg was reelected, Hitler and the Nazis had shown their power.

During the election campaigns, stormtrooper violence increased. In June and the first three weeks of July 1932, there

On January 30, 1933, Hitler became chancellor, the head of the German government. One of the most criminal and brutal governments in history came to power through a back-room deal.

were officially 461 political riots in Prussia, the largest German state. Over 80 people were killed and hundreds were seriously injured.

In July 1932, there was another election to the Reichstag. The Nazi gains were again startling. They got almost 14 million votes, and won 230 seats in the Reichstag, more than double their totals from 1930. This was about 37 percent of the votes, about the same proportion that Hitler had received for president a few months earlier. The Nazis had become the largest party in Germany. The Social Democrats dropped to less than 8 million votes and 133 seats.

Hitler makes a deal

Hitler and various conservative leaders bargained for months, trying to make a deal to join their parties so that together they would have enough votes in the Reichstag to be able to pass legislation. These leaders felt the Nazis were basically on their side, and could be useful in helping them run the country. They believed the Nazis just needed to be "tamed" a little. They convinced President Hindenburg to name Hitler as chancellor. Most of the members of the cabinet would not be Nazis, but old-fashioned conservatives. Besides Hitler, there were only two other Nazis in the cabinet, out of twelve. The conservatives stayed in charge of the army and the national police. Hitler, they were sure, would be under their control.

On January 30, 1933, Hitler became chancellor, the head of the German government. He came to power legally, though without ever winning a majority of the votes, in an agreement with conservative political leaders. One of the most criminal and brutal governments in history came to power through a back-room deal.

The end of democracy

Hitler decided to hold one more election, in March 1933, the third in less than a year. He used his increased power and his stormtroopers to ensure that the Nazis would win a majority in the Reichstag. On February 27, 1933, after Hitler

had been chancellor less than a month, the Reichstag building was set on fire. The Nazis claimed this was part of a communist plan to start a revolution. No one believes this today. Many people thought at the time that the Nazis had set the fire themselves, but there was no way to prove this.

The next day, Hitler issued an emergency decree signed by President Hindenburg. This decree gave Hitler special powers to "protect" the nation against "Communist acts of violence." It gave the government the power to ignore almost all the rights in the constitution.

Hitler could restrict freedom of speech and of the press, ban meetings, and outlaw political organizations. His police could tap telephones, open private mail, search homes without a warrant. The government could seize the property of its opponents. The decree allowed Hitler to take over the government of the different states. It was the end of democracy in Germany.

German policemen view the remains of the Reichstag building after it was destroyed by fire.
(Reproduced by permission of Bildarchiv Preussischer Kulturbesitz)

The beginning of the Nazi police state

The Nazis moved quickly. The night after the Reichstag fire, the police arrested over 10,000 people. All the leaders of the Communist Party who could be found, including members of the Reichstag, were jailed. The rest went into hiding. The arrested Communists were soon sent to concentration camps, where they were kept under guard of the Nazi stormtroopers. The Communists were the first victims of the Nazi police state.

Forty thousand Nazi stormtroopers had been made special police officers. They still wore their Nazi uniforms as they beat their opponents, kidnapped them, and spread terror everywhere. Only now they were acting legally, under Chancellor Hitler's orders. The regular police just watched.

As the election campaign continued, only pro-Nazi political meetings were allowed. The offices of anti-Nazi newspapers were smashed. The speeches of Hitler and other top Nazis filled the radio.

The last election

Almost 90 percent of the voters cast their ballots on March 5, 1933. Although Nazi control of the government and stormtrooper violence meant that the election was only partly free, voters could choose other parties. The Nazis got over 17 million votes, about 44 percent. The Nationalist Party, the allies of the Nazis in the election, got another 3 million. Much more surprising was the fact that the Social Democrats got 7 million votes, and the Communists, even though they were in jail or hiding, still received almost 5 million votes.

Even in these circumstances, a majority of Germans still refused to vote for the Nazis. A large minority, over 30 percent, voted for the two parties that the Nazis hated most, the Social Democrats and Communists. In was a serious disappointment for the Nazis. But votes did not matter anymore. The Nazis had enough power to control the government, and they used it.

A majority of Germans still refused to vote for the Nazis. But votes did not matter anymore. The Nazis had enough power to control the government, and they used it.

The Nazis take control of Germany

On March 24 1933, the new Reichstag passed a law called the Enabling Act. It allowed the government to issue laws, without the approval of the Reichstag, for four years. Unlike the emergency decree, these laws could be issued by Hitler alone, without the approval of President Hindenburg. The Enabling Act clearly said that these new laws could violate the constitution.

From now on, the "law" was whatever Adolf Hitler wanted it to be, and he could now "legally" do the things the Nazis had always intended. During the next several months, almost every organization that might oppose the Nazis was destroyed.

In April, the first law was issued to remove opponents of the Nazis from all government jobs. Soon, practicing law required Nazi approval. Within a few months, this was true for journalists, radio broadcasters, musicians, and people working in the theater.

On May 2, 1933, the stormtroopers took over the offices of all the labor unions in Germany, beat up union leaders, and sent them to concentration camps. The free labor

The German Führer

The president of Germany, Paul von Hindenburg, died in August 1934. The position of president and the position of chancellor, which Hitler already held, were now combined. Hitler was now the Führer (leader) of the German Reich (empire). He was also the commander-in-chief of the army.

On the day that Hindenburg died, every officer and soldier of the army swore a new oath of allegiance: "I swear by God this holy oath: I will give unconditional obedience to the Führer of the German Reich and People, Adolf Hitler, the Supreme Commander of the Armed Forces and will be ready, as a brave soldier, to lay down my life at any time for this oath." The German army did not promise loyalty to the German people or to the law, or even to the German government. It promised to obey Adolf Hitler.

unions were replaced by the German Labor Front, run by a Nazi official. All workers had to belong. Later that month, the workers' right to bargain with their employers, and the right to strike, were abolished.

In June, the Social Democratic Party was officially banned as "an enemy of the people." The same month, the stormtroopers took over many offices of the Nationalist Party, the Nazis' ally in the last election, and still their partner in the government. Knowing that it would soon be eliminated anyway, the Nationalist Party announced that it had dissolved. The same sort of thing happened to every other political party.

On July 14, 1933, Germany officially became a one-party state. On that day, a new law was published. It said that "the National Socialist German Workers' Party [the Nazi Party's full name] constitutes the only political Party in Germany." It also said that anyone who tried to keep another political party going, or who tried to form a new political party, could be sent to prison.

Within six months after becoming chancellor, Hitler was now the dictator of Germany. The Nazi Party was the only legal political party.

Military power for Germany

One of Hitler's goals was to make Germany a great military power again. To build up the armed forces meant that Germany would have to ignore the Treaty of Versailles, which limited Germany's army to 100,000 soldiers, did not allow a military draft, banned tanks and an air force, and kept the navy very small. In this goal, Hitler had the support of the military officers. Long before Hitler came to power, the military

had been secretly making plans to get around the treaty, doing things like training pilots on glider planes and experimenting with designs for modern tanks. Hitler expanded the rearming of Germany secretly, but he was also determined to defy the Treaty of Versailles openly.

Defying the treaty

Early in 1935, Germany announced that it would again draft men into the army. Although this violated the Treaty of Versailles, Britain and France did not do anything about it. Within weeks, Hitler announced the creation of a German air force, again violating the treaty. On March 16, Germany officially announced that it would no longer respect the t21reaty's limitations on the German armed forces.

The next year, Hitler sent the German army into the western area of Germany, near France, called the Rhineland.

Adolf Hitler honors the Condor Legion veterans after their return from Spain. These German volunteers fought on the fascist side in the Spanish Civil War.
(Reproduced by permission of Bildarchiv Preussischer Kulturbesitz)

The Rhineland was part of Germany, but according to the Treaty of Versailles, it was not supposed to have any troops in it. This move was a big gamble for Hitler. The German army was still far too weak to do anything if France tried to stop this action. The German generals tried to talk Hitler out of this step, but he believed that France and Britain would not do anything except protest—and he was right.

From 1936 to 1939, a civil war raged in Spain. A general named Francisco Franco led a rebellion against the elected government. Franco and many of his supporters were friendly to the Nazis. Hitler sent German planes and pilots to support Franco's troops. The German air force used the Spanish Civil War as a way to develop Germany's modern air warfare tactics. This included purposely bombing civilian populations. The German bombing of the town of Guernica shocked people around the world and inspired a famous painting by Pablo Picasso, "Guernica."

Germany expands without firing a shot

In March 1938, the German army moved into Austria, and Germany and Austria were united into one country. This was called the *Anschluss,* which means "union" or "joining" in German. Hitler worked with Austrian Nazis to bring about the *Anschluss,* but it was an old dream of many Germans and Austrians. Many Austrians—perhaps most—welcomed becoming part of Germany.

Hitler soon began to look for more territory. He demanded that a part of western Czechoslovakia, called the Sudetenland, become part of Germany. He claimed that Czechoslovakia was mistreating the German-speaking population of the Sudetenland. This was simply an excuse for Hitler, who was probably perterbed that German people were living under the rule of non–Germans. He had told his generals in May that "it is my unchangeable intention to destroy Czechoslovakia by military force in the foreseeable future."

The crisis over the Sudetenland came very close to starting a war. But Czechoslovakia's allies, Britain and France, were not willing to defend Czechoslovakia, which could not stand alone against Germany. Instead, in September 1938 the leaders of France, Britain, and Italy met with Hitler in Munich, a city of southern Germany. Italy's leader, Benito Mussolini, was Hitler's ally. Czechoslovakia was not allowed to attend the conference.

Appeasing a dictator

At Munich, Britain and France agreed to let Hitler take over the Sudetenland. Hitler told the British prime minister (the head of the British government), Neville Chamberlain, that this was his "last territorial demand in Europe," and Chamberlain believed him—or wanted to believe him.

The Munich Conference has become famous as the symbol of the British and French policy of appeasement, of giving in to Hitler's demands to avoid war. When Chamberlain returned to London, he waved a copy of the Munich agreement at the airport and said that he had brought home "peace in our time."

Opponents of appeasement attacked Chamberlain and the French prime minister, Edouard Daladier, for giving in to Hitler's threats. The prime ministers were so afraid of war, these critics said, that they were willing to go back on their promises and to sacrifice the people of a democratic country, Czechoslovakia, to the Nazis. In fact, the opponents said, this would make war more likely, by encouraging further demands by Hitler.

But it is important to remember that, at the time, the desire to avoid war was such a powerful feeling in Europe that appeasement was favored by most people. The German people shared this feeling as well. According to both German and foreign observers, people in Germany did not respond well to Nazi propaganda about the Czechoslovakia crisis. They did not want to go to war over the Sudetenland and—like most people in France and Britain—were immensely relieved that the issue was settled. Hitler became more popular, even among some anti-Nazi Germans, because he had shown that he could win gains for Germany without war.

Another factor contributing to appeasement was that Chamberlain and Daladier—along with their military advisers—did not think their armed forces were ready for war. Both Britain and France were rapidly building more weapons and planes and they thought that a delay would help them. Of course, Germany was also building new weapons. In hindsight, many military experts think that Britain and France would have been better off fighting Germany in the fall of 1938 rather than a year later, as actually happened.

The end of appeasement

The Munich settlement did not bring peace, of course. By March 1939, Hitler's army took over all of Czechoslovakia.

The provinces of Bohemia and Moravia (most of what is now the Czech Republic) became part of Germany. The Nazis set up an "independent" country of Slovakia, but it was really a German puppet (a country that claims to be independent but is really being controlled by another more powerful country).

The destruction of Czechoslovakia violated the Munich agreement. It showed everyone—even those who had wanted to believe otherwise—that appeasement could not work. Even Chamberlain was now determined to stop Hitler's next move, by force if necessary.

Hitler's next target was Poland. The port city of Danzig (now the Polish city of Gdansk) had been made a "free city" after World War I, which meant it was not part of Germany or Poland. Poland had a right to use the port for its exports and imports. But the people of the city were almost all German, and local Nazis ran the city and followed Hitler's orders. Germany demanded that Danzig be returned to Germany, something that most people in Danzig wanted.

Within six months of the Munich agreement, Germany had completely dismantled Czechoslovakia, taking Bohemia and Moravia for itself and turning the rest into the puppet state of Slovakia.

This demand might have seemed reasonable a few years earlier. By now, however, most people understood that giving in to Hitler's demands—even if they seemed justified at first—would only lead to more and more demands. In fact, Hitler did not want Poland to agree: he was determined to destroy Poland as an independent country. This had been one of his major goals from the beginning.

The British and French governments said they would defend their ally Poland if it were attacked by Germany. Since Britain and France had not defended Czechoslovakia, Hitler thought they would back down again. On September 1, 1939, the German army launched a full-scale attack on Poland. Britain and France declared war on Germany two days later. World War II had begun in Europe.

War in Asia

As a new war in Europe became more and more likely, another war was already being fought in Asia between Japan and China. This conflict spread to much of eastern Asia and the Pacific, and eventually became part of the world war. The causes of World War II in Asia are closely connected with the history of Japan.

Japan is an island nation located off the eastern coast of Asia. In the early 1600s, ships from Portugal and Spain began to arrive in Japan. After a short period of welcoming them, the Japanese closed off their country. For the next two centuries, Japan was almost completely isolated from other countries, including its Asian neighbors. Japanese were not allowed to leave the country. Foreigners were not welcome—neither merchants who wanted to buy and sell in Japan, nor western missionaries who wanted to convert people to their religion.

Japan is humiliated

Beginning in the 1850s, western influence was forced on the Japanese.(The United States and countries in Europe are often referred to as western countries while countries in Asia are referred to as eastern countries.) In 1853, a group of American warships commanded by Commodore Matthew Perry entered Tokyo Bay without permission of the Japanese government. The big guns of the American ships could have destroyed the city. After a year of pressure, Japan was forced to sign a treaty with the United States, allowing American ships to enter Japanese ports. Japan soon had to sign treaties with Russia, Britain, and the Netherlands as well. From then on, American and other western merchants could not be prevented from doing business in Japan.

The Japanese were humiliated and angered over the way western countries forced their will on Japan. Japan was technologically and militarily far behind Europe and the United States and many Japanese feared that the western powers would turn Japan into one of their colonies. At that time, the western nations were taking over many foreign countries, especially in Asia and Africa, and making them colonies—running them without regard to the wishes of the native people. The Japanese believed that allowing western merchants into the country was the first step in this process.

Japan becomes a modern country

To avoid being colonized, some Japanese leaders decided their country needed to become more modern. Beginning in the late 1860s, Japan changed quickly and dramatically. One important change involved the political system. The emperor, who was supposed to be the supreme ruler of the whole country, had lost all of his real power. The real ruler of Japan was the Shogun, the head of a powerful family and a kind of military dictator. While the Shogun ran the central government, great local lords controlled much of Japan. They held large areas of land and ran these domains almost as if each were a separate country. Their word was law on their own lands. Japan didn't have a national tax system or a national army.

In 1868, after years of conflict, a group of powerful local leaders were able to overthrow the Shogun in a bloody rebellion. Officially, power was returned to the emperor. In fact, the emperor still didn't make decisions. Instead, the small group of powerful leaders who had led the rebellion ran the country.

The emperor during this time was called Meiji, and the period during which he reigned (1868–1912) in Japanese his-

Beginning in the late 1860s, Japan changed quickly and dramatically.

Japan has very few natural resources. It has no oil, and petroleum was becoming more and more important in keeping a modern country going.

tory is known as the Meiji Restoration. Even though the emperor did not run the country, he continued to enjoy extraordinary prestige among the Japanese people. The emperor was a symbol of the country, and he was worshiped as a godlike creature.

In the years following the Meiji Restoration, the government was able to abolish the old system in which the lords had almost absolute power on their own lands. Many lords remained rich and still had great influence, but Japan now had a single powerful government that ruled the whole country, in the emperor's name. Soon there was a written constitution, and a legal system was organized.

Japan did not just change politically in this period. Factories were built, like those in Europe and the United States. Soon there was widespread use of steam power, electricity, railroads, a telephone system. A modern educational system was created. Most important to the new leaders, the army and the navy were modernized with new weapons, new western-style ships, and the latest military training. In many ways, Japan was becoming a country that resembled the United States and Europe more than its Asian neighbors. These developments were brought about in a matter of a few decades.

The desire for an empire

But Japan has very few natural resources. Its factories depended on getting iron and other minerals from foreign countries. It has no oil, and petroleum was becoming more and more important in keeping a modern country going. Japanese factories, and soon the whole Japanese economy, depended on turning raw materials into finished products and then selling them. Almost all the raw materials had to be imported. Many of the finished products had to be sold in other countries.

The logical place for Japan to get these resources was from the mainland of Asia. This was also the logical place for Japan to sell the products made in its factories. The western countries, Germany, France, and especially Britain, had faced some of these same problems many years earlier. One of the things they had done was to build great empires in foreign

countries (colonies) where they could use the resources of the colony for the benefit of the home country. Much of Asia was controlled directly by these western countries by the end of the nineteenth century. This was the age of "imperialism," of empire building.

Japan also wanted to control foreign countries and use them for the benefit of Japan. (Neither the western imperial powers nor Japan were interested in what the people of these countries wanted.) But because Japan was a latecomer, it was shut out of many of these countries—unless it was willing to go to war against the western powers who were already there.

Japan's first conquests

Tensions between Japan and China were increasing during the final decades of the nineteenth century, especially over the growing Japanese influence in Korea. Korea was a

Japan's new warships were a vital part of their plan to modernize the country.
(Reproduced by permission of AP/Wide World Photos)

East Asia, 1912.

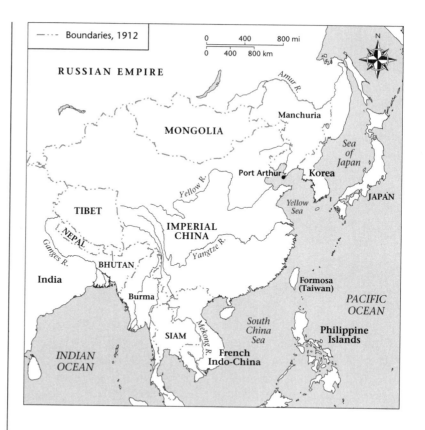

semi-independent country that for many centuries had owed allegiance to China. But China was too weak to control its outlying areas. Japan began stationing troops in Korea, despite Chinese protests.

From 1894 to 1895, Japan fought a short war with China. China was much larger than Japan, but its government was weak and unable to control the country. The newly modernized Japanese army won an easy victory and Japan forced China to give up the island of Formosa, off the southeast coast of China (today the island is called by its Chinese name, Taiwan). This was Japan's first colony. In addition, China was forced not to interfere with Japanese influence in Korea, and that country came under the "protection" of Japan. Korea essentially became a Japanese colony. Later, in 1910, Japan officially ended Korea's independence and made it part of Japan.

In the treaty that ended the war with China, Japan also demanded to make part of Manchuria, in northeast China, a colony. Manchuria is rich in coal and minerals, including iron, and its vast farmable land could grow much of the grain to help feed Japan. China was forced to agree to give up part of Manchuria, but the European powers, especially Russia, France, and Germany, did not want Japan to dominate the region. Russia even threatened to go to war with Japan if Japan exerted its control there. Though Japan was forced to give up this plan, and officially Manchuria remained part of China, Japanese influence in the region was very large and it continued to grow.

War with Russia

Russia was another country that was expanding its empire in eastern Asia at this time. The Russian Czars (emperors) had extended their territory to the Pacific Ocean, and Russia's influence, like Japan's, was growing in Manchuria. The conflict between Russia and Japan over Manchuria grew and in 1905 the two countries went to war. The war began with a surprise attack by the Japanese navy against the Russian fleet anchored in Port Arthur (or Lü-shun, on the southern Liaotung Peninsula, which jutted into the Yellow Sea). The Japanese army defeated the Russian troops in bloody fighting in Manchuria, and the Japanese navy won another sea battle, almost completely destroying a second Russian fleet.

Japan's victory in the war gave it a free hand to increase its influence and economic power in Manchuria. It also changed the way other countries in the world looked at Japan, and at the way the Japanese looked at themselves. For the first time in modern history, an Asian country had defeated a European power in a war. From then on, Japan was considered one of the military and naval powers. It even joined France, Britain, and the United States in World War I and took over several German-controlled islands in the Pacific Ocean.

In the following decades, Japanese power and influence continued to grow. Japanese companies owned railroads and coal mines in Manchuria and controlled the area's economic policies. Japanese troops were stationed there to protect these interests. Officially, however, Manchuria was still part of China. In 1931, the Japanese army in Manchuria—without the permission of the Japanese government—seized

By the 1930s, Japan was in many ways coming to resemble the fascist governments of Italy and Nazi Germany.

Manchuria in a short war with China. Japanese troops burned villages, shot Chinese civilians, and raped Chinese women. The Japanese army then set up a new country, and named it Manchukuo. Although it was supposed to be an independent country, with a Chinese emperor and its own government, the government was really under Japan's control. The commander of the Japanese troops stationed in Manchukuo made all the key decisions.

Militarism in the government

The attack on Manchuria, which began without the permission or even the knowledge of the Japanese government, was evidence of a another great change taking place in Japan. The leaders of the army and navy were becoming more and more important in running the country. Younger military officers also played a significant part in Japanese politics. They helped organize secret patriotic societies, some of them with tens of thousands of members. These organizations wanted Japan to increase its military and naval forces, they wanted Japan to seize a larger empire, and they were against a democratic political system. Sometimes they assassinated civilian politicians who did not agree with them.

By the 1930s, Japan was in many ways coming to resemble the fascist governments of Italy and Nazi Germany. Fascism is a political movement marked by extreme nationalism, celebration of military strength, strong anticommunism, and a belief in a single all-powerful leader. (The fascist governments of Europe are discussed on pages 10–13.) In Japan, the whole country was under the influence of the army and its traditions. The old warrior tradition of Japan was glorified; the ancestors of many Japanese military officers were samurai, the Japanese warriors of the middle ages (from about 500 to 1500 A.D.). Worship of the emperor as a descendant of the gods became more prominent in Japanese religion. Schoolchildren were taught that dying for the emperor was the greatest honor for a Japanese person, and that obedience to the emperor's wishes was both a religious and patriotic duty.

In fact, it was not the emperor's orders that the people were following, but the orders of the military men and their allies, who were really making the decisions. Limits were placed on what could be printed in newspapers and magazines; the labor unions lost all their power; and college students were forced to memorize information fed to them by their professors instead of being encouraged to think for themselves. Women were discouraged from playing any part in society outside their traditional roles of wives and mothers.

The whole country was being organized to support the ideas and goals of the militarists, extremists in the military and their supporters who wanted Japan to be controlled by the army, and wanted all of Japanese society organized on military principles. Any disagreement with the government's policies was considered unpatriotic, even a crime. The secret police became a powerful body, with spies everywhere. Politicians who did not support the army strongly enough, and even some generals who were considered too moderate by younger army officers, were in constant fear of being murdered by the secret societies. In February 1936, hundreds of armed junior military officers took over the center of Tokyo. They found and killed several leading antimilitarist politicians. After this, the militarists' influence in the government increased even more.

The militarists openly expressed their dislike of foreigners and a belief that the Japanese were a superior race of people. Influences from Europe and the United States, things like western-style ballroom dancing and English-language street signs, were attacked. At the same time, Japanese militarists began talking about driving out the western powers from Asia. They advanced the idea that the people of these countries should run their own affairs and used the slogan "Asia for the Asians." But Japanese treatment of Manchukuo and Korea made it clear that the Japanese militarists did not really want to make Asian nations independent: they wanted Japan to take control of the Asian countries. Even so, the idea of getting rid of the western imperial powers, with Japan's help, attracted many Asian people, at least at first.

The militarists openly expressed their dislike of foreigners and a belief that the Japanese were a superior race of people.

Conflict and alliance with the West

The creation of Manchukuo created conflicts with other countries, especially the United States. The American government refused to recognize Manchukuo, demanding that it be returned to China. The United States arranged for bank loans to the Chinese government to make it stronger, and began selling planes to the Chinese air force. The tensions between the United States and Japan over China would continue to grow, and would eventually lead to war.

In November 1936, Japan signed a treaty with Nazi Germany, with the two countries pledging to oppose the spread of the world communist movement. (Communism is a political and economic system where most property is owned in common by the community as a whole.) Partly this treaty reflected the changes in Japan and the militarists' admiration of Nazi Germany. The Nazis also opposed democracy, glorified military might, and wanted to take over new territory. But the treaty was also directed at Russia, Japan's old rival in Manchuria, which was now the Communist-ruled Soviet Union. The Soviet leaders now had to worry that Germany and Japan might attack Russia from two sides, thousands of miles apart.

War against China

But Japan did not attack the Soviet Union. Instead, it turned south from Manchuria. In July 1937, Japan invaded China itself. Japanese troops attacked and conquered large areas of the country, including the great cities of Peking (now Beijing), Shanghai, and Canton. As they had in 1931, the Japanese soldiers were allowed—perhaps even encouraged—to burn villages, loot (steal) property, and to rape and murder Chinese civilians. The most terrible example was what the victorious Japanese army did in the city of Nanking. After conquering the city on December 13, the Japanese troops went on a rampage. They dragged thousands of people out of their homes and shot or bayonetted them. Others were burned alive. Women were repeatedly sexually attacked. The slaughter became known as the "rape of Nanking." At least 40,000 Chinese were killed.

Although the Chinese armies sometimes fought hard, they could not stop the Japanese from conquering large areas of China, including all the important seaports. Japan controlled most of the railroads and much of the most important farming and industrial areas of China. But the Japanese troops were not able to advance inland into the great spaces of China.

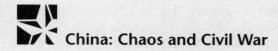

China: Chaos and Civil War

One of the reasons that Japan was able to defeat the Chinese so easily in battle during the first half of the twentieth century was that China was embroiled in an ongoing civil war. In 1912 the old Chinese Empire was overthrown and a republic was established. The old government had become weaker and weaker and very corrupt. Its authority was very limited and much of China was ruled by powerful warlords (military leaders who take control of a region and hold power by force). The private armies of the warlords terrorized the poor peasants (farmers who own little or no land of their own), taking their crops, demanding high taxes, and forcing their sons into their armies. The new government of the republic, known as the Nationalists (or Kuomintang in Chinese), took many years to defeat these warlords, and it had not completely succeeded by the time Japan invaded.

Meanwhile, the Nationalist government was itself full of corruption, sometimes making alliances with warlords and seeming to favor the tiny minority of rich Chinese at the expense of the millions of poor—often starving—peasants. Opponents of the Nationalists formed a Chinese communist party that soon gained much support among the poor. Among other things, it promised to take over the land and give it to the peasants. Sometimes Communist soldiers would publicly shoot landlords to show the peasants that the Communists, unlike the Nationalists, were the enemies of the rich.

For a while the Nationalists and Communists had been allies. But soon they were bitter enemies, and the Nationalist army tried to destroy the Communists. When Japan attacked, the Communists proposed that the two Chinese parties join forces against the invaders. But many Nationalists thought this was only a trick for the Communists to gain more support. Throughout the war with Japan, Chiang Kai-Shek, the leader of the Nationalists, was much more concerned about defeating the Communists than in fighting the Japanese. He used some of his best troops to keep the Communist armies isolated. During the eight years that China fought Japan, the civil war between the Nationalists and Communists was sometimes pushed into the background, with limited cooperation between the two sides. After the defeat of Japan in 1945, it again became a full-scale war, until the Communists won complete control of the country in 1949.

China was simply too big, and the Japanese did not have enough soldiers. Sometimes protected by mountains, the Chinese armies continued to exist. Sometimes they launched guerrilla raids on the Japanese.

By the end of 1938, after a year and a half of heavy fighting, the war between Japan and China settled into a kind of holding pattern. The Japanese did not try to launch major operations to attack the remaining Chinese armies. The Chinese were not able to counterattack and win back the territories that Japan had conquered. Although many soldiers and civilians continued to die, and the Chinese people in the Japanese controlled areas suffered tremendous hardships, there were no more large-scale battles for many years.

This was the situation in eastern Asia at the moment that Europe went to war in September 1939. The Japanese war against China was still a separate war from the one that began in Europe. The two conflicts would become a single world war in late 1941.

The Beginning of the War in Europe

2

Soon after Germany took over Czechoslovakia in March 1939 (see Chapter 1), it began to make demands on Poland. Nazi dictator Adolf Hitler demanded that the city of Danzig, a port on the Baltic Sea, be returned to Germany. Danzig (now the Polish city of Gdansk) had been made a "free city" after World War I, which meant it was not part of Germany or Poland. Poland, which then had no other ports, had the right to use Danzig for its exports and imports, which made the city very important to the Polish economy. But the people of the city were almost all German, and the local Nazis ran the city and followed Hitler's orders.

In addition, Hitler wanted the right to build a road across the "Polish Corridor," the slice of Polish territory that separated the German province of East Prussia from the rest of Germany. The proposed road would be German territory.

Even if the Polish government had been willing to surrender these lands, it believed that they were only excuses and that Germany would only demand more. The governments of Britain and France felt the same way. In fact, Hitler did not want Poland to agree to the demands: from the begin-

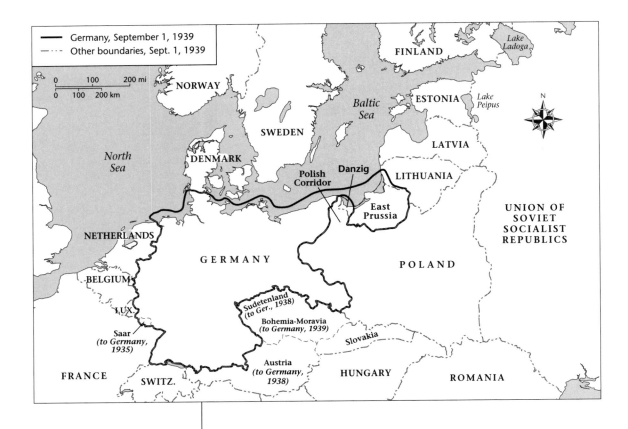

Adolf Hitler's early demands for territory concerned the port city of Danzig and the Polish Corridor, land that Germany lost after World War I.

ning he had been determined to destroy Poland as an independent country.

The German demands caused a crisis throughout the summer of 1939. The leaders of Britain and France were now determined to resist Germany by force if it attempted to seize any more territory. Britain and France began to negotiate with the Soviet Union (Russia and the territory it controlled), Poland's eastern neighbor, trying to extract an agreement to defend Poland. But the Polish government was just as suspicious of the Soviets as it was of Germany. Poland knew that the Soviet Union wanted large parts of eastern Poland, where the majority of the people were not Polish, to become Soviet territory. The suspicion was increased because the Soviet government was communist, and the Polish government was strongly anticommunist. (In theory, communism is a political and economic system in which most property is owned in common by the community. The Soviet Union was, by 1939, a harsh dictatorship run by the Communist Party and its all-powerful leader, Joseph Stalin.)

Poland absolutely refused to allow Soviet troops to enter Polish territory if Germany attacked Poland. The Poles were afraid that the troops would never leave. But without this condition, a Soviet agreement to help defend Poland was worthless. The French and British negotiations with the Soviet Union dragged on, but they made little progress.

The Nazi-Soviet Pact

Meanwhile, the Soviet Union was involved in secret discussions with Nazi Germany. On August 23, 1939, the two countries signed the Nazi-Soviet Pact (also called the Molotov-Ribbentrop pact). The treaty shocked everyone. Nazi Germany had claimed to be the greatest enemy of communism and the Soviet government. The Soviet Union had always called the Nazis brutal murderers and enemies of the workers, whom the communists claimed to represent.

For Hitler, the treaty meant that Germany could invade Poland without having to fight Soviet troops. Hitler did not think that Britain and France would actually go to war to defend Poland. But he wanted to make sure that, if they did, Germany would not face powerful enemies on two sides at the same time.

The reasons Stalin agreed to the treaty are more complicated. Soviet leaders claimed afterward that the treaty was intended to "buy time" to prepare for a war against the Nazis—a war they said they knew would come someday.

Stalin—like Hitler—doubted that Britain and France would fight Germany and suspected that they really wanted Hitler to attack the Soviet Union. The Nazi-Soviet Pact ended that threat, at least for the time being. The Soviet Union also feared war with Japan. At the time, Soviet and Japanese forces were engaged in vicious battles along the far eastern border of the Soviet Union. Like the Germans, the Soviets wanted to eliminate any chance that they would have to fight a war on two sides.

However, these defensive considerations were not Stalin's only reasons. Germany secretly agreed in the treaty to

For Hitler, the Nazi-Soviet Pact meant that Germany could invade Poland without having to fight Soviet troops. For Stalin, the treaty ended the threat of the Germans attacking the Soviet Union, at least for the time being.

Molotov Vyacheslav Mikhaylovich, prime minister of the Soviet Union, signing the Nazi-Soviet nonaggression pact. *(Reproduced by permission of Bildarchiv Preussischer Kulturbesitz)*

give the Soviet Union a large part of eastern Poland and let them take over the nearby countries of Lithuania, Latvia, and Estonia. The treaty meant Stalin could wait until Germany destroyed the Polish army to take over eastern Poland. And if the Soviets really intended the pact as a defensive measure against Nazi Germany, it is hard to explain the fact that the Soviet Union helped Germany in many important ways in the twenty-two months between the signing of the pact and the German surprise invasion of the Soviet Union in June 1941.

The beginning of the war

Although the British and French governments were not happy about the Nazi-Soviet Pact, they convinced themselves that it did not change things drastically. Their generals believed that the Soviet army was not a powerful force and that it might not have been much help anyway. They also greatly overestimated the strength of the Polish army. Although they did not believe that Poland could defeat Germany, they thought it could hold out long enough for the British and French to attack Germany from the west and for their air forces to inflict serious damage. The Polish government and military leaders were also counting on a great offensive by the French army into western Germany.

Hitler, however, gambled that his armies could defeat Poland before France and Britain were ready to fight. The German army stationed only about 40 divisions on the border with France. (A division is a large unit of an army, usually about 15,000 men.) The French army supposedly had 100 divisions, though most of the soldiers were in the reserves, leading civilian lives, and had not yet been mobilized (called to active duty in the army.)

Most of the German forces were therefore free to attack Poland. More than 60 divisions were involved, including 6 armored divisions and 10 mechanized divisions. An armored division is based on tanks. German tanks were called Panzers, and an armored division was called a Panzer division. A mechanized division is one in which the soldiers are supplied with trucks and other motorized transportation, sometimes including light armored vehicles with cannons or machine guns mounted on them. In regular infantry divisions, the soldiers might travel to the war zone on trains. But once there, they traveled on foot. Their food and ammunition supplies were usually carried in horse-drawn wagons. Their artillery pieces (cannons) might be on wheels, but they too were pulled by horses. Unlike tanks, which can cross open

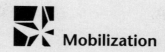

Mobilization

Mobilization is when a country calls up its reserves, the soldiers who have been trained during their army duty but are no longer on active service. In most European countries at the beginning of World War II, every healthy young man was drafted into the armed forces. After serving one or two years as a full-time soldier, he was then required to remain in the reserves for many years. Some reserves went on active duty for a week or two each year for further training.

This reserves system allowed the army to grow tremendously when the country went to war. However, mobilization seriously disrupted the economy by taking millions of men away from their jobs. In the summer of 1939, fear of damaging its already weak economy caused Poland to delay mobilization, which was still incomplete when Germany invaded.

Mobilization also forces potential enemies to mobilize *their* forces, therefore making war more likely. For these reasons, mobilization is not done lightly.

This new strategy, based on speed and mobility and using tanks fighting together in large groups (instead of scattered among infantry units), became known as blitzkrieg, or "lightning war."

fields, units depending on horse-drawn transport had to travel on roads, which the enemy could more easily defend. In World War II, even the German army, which was considered highly modern and mechanized, still depended on horses for most of its transportation needs in battle.

A new theory of warfare

Although the tank units were only a small part of the German army, they made the difference in the first year of World War II. Armored and mechanized divisions can move much more quickly than regular infantry units. Even more important, armored divisions are very difficult for infantry to stop. If commanded correctly, armored units can cut through defensive positions manned by infantry and advance far into enemy territory, circling behind defensive positions and cutting off the enemy army from its supplies and reinforcements. This was what the German generals intended to do in Poland. The Polish forces would be stranded and eventually destroyed by the German infantry divisions that followed the Panzer divisions.

The Germans also had more than 1,300 modern planes, including fighters and dive-bombers, ready for the attack on Poland. Their job was to attack Polish ground troops resisting the tanks. The dive-bombers could swoop down to a low altitude and release their bombs against antitank artillery emplacements (positions) and the few Polish tanks. The Panzer divisions and the air force were supposed to work together closely.

This was a new kind of warfare that various military thinkers had proposed in the years after World War I. British military writers had originated some of these ideas, but only German generals decided to base their strategy on these principles. This new strategy, based on speed and mobility and using tanks fighting together in large groups (instead of scattered among infantry units), became known as *blitzkrieg,* or "lightning war." (Although the word is German, it was invented by Western newspapers to describe the German army's actions in Poland.)

The Polish army would become the first victim of the blitzkrieg. The Poles had 40 divisions, but none was armored. The few Polish tanks were much older than the Germans' and

more lightly armored. The most mobile and fastest units in the Polish army were old-fashioned cavalry (horse-mounted troops). The Polish air force included more than 900 planes, but only half of them were modern; the rest were no match for the Germans.

The Poles also faced a problem of geography. The German province of East Prussia was directly north of central Poland. The territory of Slovakia, a newly "independent" country that was actually controlled by Germany, cut deeply along Poland's southern border. And the main part of Germany was directly to Poland's west. In other words, German troops could attack Poland from three directions.

Blitzkrieg

Late on August 31, 1939, Germany claimed that some Polish troops had crossed the border and attacked German sol-

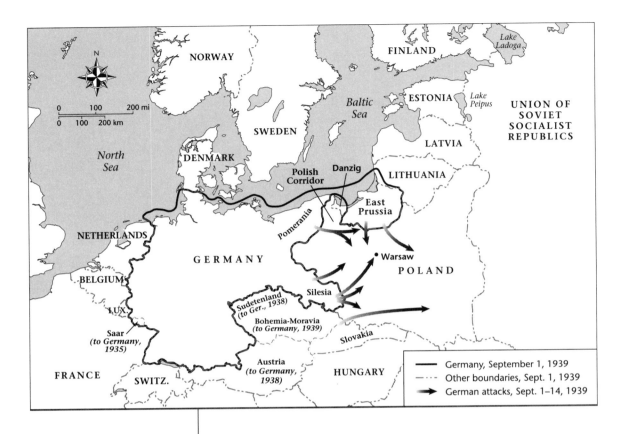

In 1939, Germany was in position to attack Poland on three sides: from Germany in the west, from the German province of East Prussia in the north, and from German-friendly Slovakia in the south.

diers. They even displayed the bodies of "Polish soldiers" killed in the fighting. In fact, there had been no attack by Poland, and the bodies were those of prisoners from a concentration camp (the brutal prison camps where the Nazis sent their opponents) who had been dressed in Polish uniforms and shot.

With this excuse, which no one believed, Germany invaded Poland before dawn on September 1, 1939. The German air force (*Luftwaffe* in German) almost wiped out the Polish air force on the first day of fighting. Many of the Polish planes were destroyed on their airfields before they even got off the ground. The German tanks pushed quickly into Polish territory. Within two days, the German troops moving south from East Prussia reached those moving east from the main part of Germany. After less than a week, one German army had fought all the way through southwestern Poland and was within 40 miles of Warsaw, the Polish capital. Another German army, which had moved south from East Prussia, was even closer. By September 17, Warsaw was surrounded, and the Luftwaffe bombed it heavily, causing a great many civilian deaths, until the city surrendered on September 27.

By mid-September, the Polish army's only chance to survive as a fighting force—and it was not a very good chance—was to retreat to the east and try to establish a defensive position near the Soviet border. But on September 17, the Soviet army invaded Poland from the east, as the secret part of the Nazi-Soviet Pact provided. More than 200,000 retreating Polish troops had no choice but to surrender to the Soviet army. Farther west, some Polish units continued to fight the Germans, but by early October, the battle for Poland was over.

The blitzkrieg had gone exactly as planned. The Polish divisions were unable to react to the German army's speed. The Polish troops generally fought with great bravery, but they had no planes to attack the German tanks or to defend themselves against the Luftwaffe. They were outnumbered and had fewer and poorer weapons. More than 100,000 Polish soldiers died in the short war, and the Germans captured about 700,000 more.

Continuing the Battle

After the Germans invaded Poland in September 1939, about 100,000 Polish troops managed to escape to neighboring countries and eventually reached France or Britain. Many of them continued to fight against Germany in special Polish units for the rest of the war. Many Polish pilots flew in Britain's Royal Air Force and participated in the Battle of Britain. Among many other places, Polish troops fought at Monte Casino in Italy and in Normandy in France. (The Battle of Britain is described later in this chapter, the fighting in Italy in Chapter 10, and the invasion of Normandy in Chapter 11.)

The Polish government also escaped to Britain. Throughout the war, most of the countries that fought Germany considered it the official and legal government of Poland.

About 14,000 Germans were killed and another 30,000 wounded. By the bloody standards of the war that had now begun, Hitler's first military conquest had been quick and easy.

The "phony war"

Hitler was surprised when Britain and France (known as the "Allies") declared war after he invaded Poland in 1939. He thought they would do nothing, as they had when he took over Czechoslovakia. He knew that they could not help Poland militarily and thought the declaration of war was only for

The British had always had a small army. It's air force and navy, however, were among the most powerful in the world.

show. During the fighting in Poland, the French had launched only a minor attack into Germany—nothing like the major offensive that Poland had needed and the German generals had feared.

With Poland defeated so quickly, Germany could transfer its army to the French-German border. But Hitler did not want to attack France yet. Instead, he believed that he could end the war immediately by promising—again—that he would never attack another country if Britain and France would accept Germany's conquest of Poland.

But Britain and France insisted, both publicly and in private discussions with various "unofficial" German representatives, that there could be peace only if Germany withdrew from Poland and restored Czechoslovakia's independence. They also said that no peace was possible as long as Hitler ran Germany.

In the months following Poland's defeat, there was almost no fighting on the border between France and Germany. Partly this was because the conditions in late fall and winter, when the roads and fields are muddy, were considered too difficult. But it was also because the British and French wanted as much time as possible to build more weapons and buy them from the United States. The British, who had always had a small army and had only recently started to draft men into service, needed time to build up their forces. 99The British air force and navy, however, were among the most powerful in the world.

Germany prepared during this time as well, shifting its armored divisions from Poland and building tanks and planes. Hitler hoped the delay would encourage his enemies to end the war, believing that public opinion in France and Britain would take the attitude that there was no longer any sense in fighting to defend Poland after it had already been conquered. Indeed, the people of Britain and France did question what was happening. The British called this period "the phony war"; in France it was known as the "drôle de guerre" ("a funny kind of war").

Sea battles

There was fighting at sea, however. The arms and equipment that Britain and France bought from the United

States had to be sent across the Atlantic on merchant ships. (Although refusing to join the war, the United States was openly friendly to Britain and France and openly hostile to Nazi Germany.) German submarines, known as U-boats (because the German word for "submarine" is *unterseeboots*), began to attack and sink these ships. Allied naval vessels protected them and tried to destroy the U-boats. This key struggle, which continued for years, became known as "the Battle of the Atlantic." (The Battle of the Atlantic is described in Chapter 3.)

The German navy relied on submarines much more than other countries. It had relatively few surface warships, which the powerful British navy made a determined effort to hunt down and sink. During the months of the "phony war," British naval victories encouraged the people at home, who needed to be shown that, despite what happened in Poland, Germany could be defeated. The most spectacular example was the chase of the *Graf Spee,* a German "pocket battleship," a ship that is smaller than a battleship but has the same large cannons. The *Graf Spee* was one of the "showpieces" of the German navy, and it had terrorized Allied ships. After a series of naval battles, three British warships finally cornered the *Graf Spee* in the harbor of Montevideo, Uruguay, on the Atlantic coast of South America. Because Uruguay was a neutral country, according to the rules of warfare it would have to intern (confine) any ship that stayed in its port too long. This kept neutral countries from favoring one country over another. So the *Graf Spee* either had to leave soon and face the warships or stay in Montevideo for the rest of the war. Faced with this choice, the crew of the *Graf Spee* blew their ship up as it sailed out of the harbor on December 13, 1939.

The German navy relied on submarines much more than other countries. It had relatively few surface warships, which the powerful British navy made a determined effort to hunt down and sink.

The invasion of Norway and Denmark

When the war on land resumed, one of the main reasons had to do with the German navy. It wanted seaports from which its ships could easily get to the Atlantic. (It was difficult to get to the ocean from Germany's own ports, on the Baltic and North Seas, without being seen—and attacked—by the British navy.) To get these ports, the commander of the navy argued for an invasion of Norway.

The need for ocean ports led Germany to attack Norway. Their primary goal was the port of Narvik, in the north of the country. The Germans attacked Denmark at the same time to make taking control of Norway easier.

Another reason had to do with iron ore, the metal used to make steel and therefore one of the most important materials for a country at war. Germany bought much of its iron ore from Sweden. During the winter, the Swedish ports were frozen, so ships could not sail to Germany. But the Norwegian port of Narvik is ice-free all year, so Swedish ore could be shipped by train to Narvik and then by boat to Germany.

Hitler and his generals decided to conquer Norway. They also decided to attack Denmark because it would make control of Norway easier. Both Denmark and Norway were neutral countries, but Germany attacked them anyway on April 9, 1940.

The tiny Danish army offered almost no resistance, and after the Germans threatened to bomb the capital city of Copenhagen, Denmark quickly surrendered.

In Norway, the Germans faced a much harder time. Partly this was because, unlike the flat farmlands of Denmark,

Norway largely consists of rugged mountainous areas. The Germans did have total surprise in their favor when the ships carrying their troops reached the Norwegian ports. They were able to seize the main ports and airfields, though the old cannon defending the Norwegian capital of Oslo sank the *Blücher,* one of the few battleships in the German navy.

The Allies sent a force of 12,000 men to help the Norwegian army. The British navy sank all ten German destroyers (a warship smaller than a battleship or cruiser) sent to the port of Narvik, which meant the entire German navy had only ten modern destroyers left. In addition, the only two German battleships left in the fleet were heavily damaged by British submarines and were out of action for the rest of the year.

Despite these defeats, the Germans completed their conquest of Norway. The British and French troops pulled out, partly because the Luftwaffe controlled the skies. But there was another reason: the troops were desperately needed elsewhere. The "phony war" had ended, and German tanks were sweeping through France.

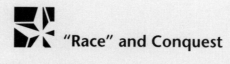

"Race" and Conquest

Although the decision to attack Norway and Denmark was originally based on military and naval considerations, it also fit into Nazi ideas about "race." The Nazis considered Germans a superior "race" who were entitled to rule over others. The Norwegians and Danes are descended from the same ancient tribes as the Germans, and their languages have the same ancestor. In Nazi thinking, this meant that these fellow "Nordic" (northern) people should be part of the Germanic empire that the Nazis wanted to build. Taking over Norway and Denmark, many Nazis thought, was like returning a long-lost cousin to the family.

In fact, the Norwegians and Danes, with very few exceptions, wanted no part of Hitler, the Nazis, or Germany. Their democratic traditions, dislike of war, and belief in tolerance were much more important to them than any supposed "racial" relationship.

The invasion of the west

Seven months after Poland's defeat, the German armies attacked in the west. On May 10, 1940, Germany invaded the Netherlands (often called Holland; in English, the people are called Dutch), Belgium, and Luxembourg, all of them neutral in the war. In the Netherlands, the attack began with parachute troops and glider-carried units landing behind the Dutch army's defensive lines. (Gliders are planes without motors towed by

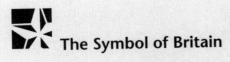

The Symbol of Britain

One result of the failure to save Norway was Neville Chamberlain's resignation as British prime minister, the head of the government. Before the war, Chamberlain had been the symbol of "appeasement," of giving in to Hitler's demands. (Appeasement is discussed in Chapter 1.)

The new prime minister was Winston Churchill. Churchill soon became a different kind of symbol. He represented, to the British people and to the rest of the world, the British determination to continue to fight Hitler, no matter what sacrifices were required. His memorable speeches stirred people, and his bulldog look of defiance made them more determined. When he flashed the "V for Victory" sign that he made famous, they could feel his confidence in their ultimate triumph.

ropes behind regular planes, and then cut loose and allowed to float down to land.) Then the German armored forces rolled over the border to join them. The small Dutch army was soon overwhelmed, and the Netherlands were already negotiating their surrender when the Luftwaffe bombed and destroyed the center of the great Dutch port of Rotterdam on May 14, killing many civilians. The Dutch army surrendered the next day, while the queen and the government fled to England.

The German attack in Belgium included 600 tanks manned by veterans of the war in Poland. The Belgian army tried to fight them in the eastern part of the country. The Allies believed this would be the main German attack towards France. A large French force consisting of the First and Seventh Armies, along with the small British force in France (called the British Expeditionary Force, or BEF), moved into Belgium to meet the Germans. The French force included some of their best troops and had some mechanized divisions. The BEF had almost no tanks. Although the Allies outnumbered the Germans in Belgium, the Germans had a great advantage in armor and speed. What was even more important, however, was that the Allied advance into Belgium was a trap. The main German offensive would come farther south, cutting off the Allied troops in Belgium.

This attack was through the Ardennes Forest, in the southern part of the French-Belgian border. To the north of the Ardennes is the flat plain of Flanders, where the French and BEF had advanced into Belgium. To the south was the Maginot line (pronounced ma-jhee-no, and named after a former cabinet member in charge of national defense). This was an immense system of powerful fortifications that the French had built to stop any German attack. The Maginot line included cannons

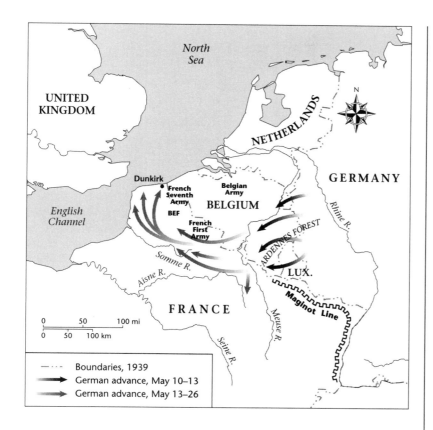

The German army surprised the Allies by driving their tanks through the Ardennes Forest and past France's Maginot line.

and machine guns inside concrete blockhouses connected by a vast system of tunnels. The French troops who manned the Maginot line could live for months in their underground shelters, safe from enemy bullets, shells, or bombs. But the Maginot line stopped at the Ardennes.

The Ardennes was heavily forested, with steep hills and very narrow roads. French military experts did not believe that large numbers of tanks could get through it, so the French side of the border was defended by only a few divisions of second-rate troops.

The Panzer breakthrough

But the Germans sent 7 armored divisions, with 1,800 tanks, through the Ardennes and into France. They made it across the Meuse River, an important natural obstacle, against strong French resistance. Once large numbers of German tanks had crossed the river, some of the French troops began to panic,

The Maginot Line

After Germany defeated France, the Maginot line became a symbol of what was wrong with French military thinking. France spent a large part of its defense budget on building it, instead of planes and tanks. It was designed to fight the kind of battles that were typical of World War I and placed the French completely on the defensive. The troops who manned it were safe—but they were also trapped. They had no way of leaving their positions and attacking the enemy, except on foot. In 1940, the Germans knew they could not attack the Maginot line directly, so they went around it. When France surrendered, the 400,000 troops assigned to the line were still there. Although they had never been defeated by the Germans, they had played no real part in defending France. The powerful cannons, pointing toward Germany, had been useless.

and the French defensive positions crumbled. The constant German air attacks, especially the dive-bombers, played a key role in destroying the confidence of the French troops.

Although the gap in the French defenses was not yet very wide, the German armored divisions poured through it and drove west and north, along the Somme River, toward the English Channel coast of France. The French troops could not stop them, and the French military command failed to organize any plan that might have saved the army. There was poor coordination between the French and the British, between the Allies and the Belgians, between the French army and the air force, and even between different parts of the French army.

Afterward, almost everyone believed that the Germans had more troops, tanks, and planes than the Allies. Although the German army did have some important advantages in weapons, this was not really the reason for its victory. In fact, in many categories, the Allies had as much equipment, and sometimes it was of higher quality. But they did not use it well. They rarely used their tanks together, instead assigning them in small groups to support infantry divisions. They did not use the air force to support armored and infantry attacks. The defeat of the French army in 1940 was, above all, a defeat of the French generals.

When the German armored divisions reached the coast, they split the French army in two. South of the Somme River, the retreating units had taken heavy casualties and needed to be reorganized. On the other side of the German tank "corridor," the French troops in Belgium, along with the BEF and the Belgian army, were being pushed south. They were now trapped between the two German forces, unable to join up with the rest of the French forces.

Dunkirk

On May 20, the same day the German tanks reached the sea, the British government began planning to evacuate the BEF to England. The BEF, along with the French First Army, began to retreat toward the coast, around the English Channel port of Dunkirk, a few miles inside France from the Belgian border. On May 26, some of the British troops boarded boats for the trip back to England. The following day, the Belgian army, now north of Dunkirk, surrendered. In the next few days, a large number of ships from England reached Dunkirk. They included not only navy ships and merchant vessels but also small fishing boats and even pleasure boats brought across the Channel by their owners. Each day, more troops boarded the boats and sailed to England. Then the boats would come back for more.

During the evacuation, the German army continually tried to fight its way into the Dunkirk "pocket," the area

With the German army approaching on all sides, the British Expeditionary Force retreated to Dunkirk and prepared for evacuation. *(Reproduced by permission of the Corbis Corporation [Bellevue])*

After the Allied evacuation from Dunkirk, Winston Churchill noted that while many lives had been saved, "wars are not won by evacuations." *(Reproduced by permission of the Corbis Corporation [Bellevue])*

defended by Allied troops. The British and French held them back long enough so that most could escape. The Luftwaffe bombed and machine-gunned the troops and the boats, but the planes of Britain's Royal Air Force (the RAF), flying from bases in England, offered some protection. The evacuation continued until June 4, with more than 300,000 Allied troops, about two-thirds of them British, brought safely to England. But they left behind almost all their equipment. (Most of the

110,000 French soldiers then went back to ports in western France, to join the French troops still fighting.)

Many people in Britain hailed Dunkirk as a great victory, calling it a "miracle." Two hundred thousand British soldiers had been saved from becoming German prisoners. But the British prime minister (the head of the government), Winston Churchill, reminded them that "wars are not won by evacuations."

The fall of France

There were still 60 divisions of French troops, though the 3 remaining armored divisions had lost many of their tanks. The Germans had 104 divisions, including 10 armored and 5 mechanized. The Luftwaffe now far outnumbered the remaining Allied planes.

Although defeat appeared certain, the French troops now fought with much greater determination. Many examples of extraordinary bravery occurred, as even the German generals admitted. The French generals finally seemed to have come up with sensible defensive plans. These plans might have worked a few weeks earlier, but now it was too late.

On June 10, the Italian dictator Benito Mussolini declared war on France and Britain and sent troops into the southern part of France. Although badly outnumbered, the four French divisions that met this new invasion easily stopped the Italians. Even so, it meant France faced another large army entering its territory.

On the same day, the French government left Paris and declared it an "open city." This meant the city would not be defended and therefore would not be bombed or destroyed in ground fighting. The German army entered the city unopposed four days later.

Hundreds of thousands of people had already left Paris, trying to escape the advancing Germans. Throughout France, roads were jammed with millions of refugees (people escaping from danger or persecution), making it even harder for the French troops to get where they were needed. Often, Luftwaffe planes machine-gunned the columns of refugees, adding to the panic and confusion.

Hitler laughs and dances a jig after the French signed the armistice ending their involvement in the war.
(Reproduced by permission of AP/Wide World Photos)

The French government now named a new prime minister: Marshal Phillippe Pétain, a hero of World War I. Pétain had helped defeat the Germans in 1918, but now he was an old man of eighty-four. He immediately asked Germany for an armistice, an end to the fighting. In the meantime, the Germans continued to advance farther into France.

On June 22, 1940, the French agreed to an armistice, effective on June 25. Hitler arranged for it to be signed in the same railroad car in the same forest clearing in which Germany had signed the armistice ending World War I, almost twenty-two years earlier. This was Hitler's special revenge on France. Once the French representatives had signed, Hitler danced a little jig outside the railroad car.

The terms of the armistice also revealed Hitler's hatred. France was divided into two parts. The German army occupied the northern half and all of the Atlantic coast, while southeastern France was occupied by Italy. Pétain's French government controlled the remainder of southern France. France had to pay for the huge cost of the German occupation, millions of dollars a day. Germany refused to release the 2 million French soldiers taken prisoner in battle. About one-quarter of all young Frenchmen were prisoners.

From the beginning of the invasion on May 10 to the end of the fighting on June 25, France had lost 90,000 people—on average, about 2,000 had died each day. Twenty-seven thousand Germans had been killed. The French army, which had been considered the strongest in the world, had been shattered in six weeks. The complete victory of Hitler's Germany seemed certain.

The Battle of Britain

Now Britain was the only country left fighting Germany. Hitler hoped that Britain would make peace, accepting the German domination of Europe in return for a promise that Germany would not interfere with Britain and its great overseas empire. The British government never seriously considered this possibility. Instead, it prepared to defend the country against a German invasion.

Invading Britain meant sending troops across the English Channel on boats. This was impossible as long as the British navy controlled the sea. Hitler hoped that the Luftwaffe could destroy the British navy from the air, but this was also impossible as long as the RAF (Britain's Royal Air Force) could fight the German planes.

So what became known as the Battle of Britain was an air battle. The German air attacks on Britain had two main purposes. One was to destroy the RAF so that an invasion could then take place. The other was to make the British people feel that there was no chance of victory and force Britain to make peace without an invasion.

Starting on July 10, 1940 and continuing for almost a month, fleets of German bombers, protected by fighter planes, attacked the ports of southern England. The RAF and land-based antiaircraft guns shot down about 100 bombers and another 80 fighters, losing around 70 fighter planes themselves. The raids did not seriously damage the British navy.

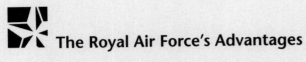

The Royal Air Force's Advantages

Although the German and British fighter planes were about equal in quality (they had similar top speeds and weapons), the British had several advantages. First, they were flying near home, so they could stay in the air much longer than the Germans, who ran out of fuel after only a short time over England.

Second, they had an excellent early warning system to spot the German planes. This system included thousands of observers along the coast, but it also depended on a chain of radar stations on the ground that warned of the number, direction, speed, and altitude of the Luftwaffe. (Neither side had yet developed radar that could fit into the planes themselves.) The system meant the British could send planes from other areas to defend that day's targets.

Another British advantage, which the Germans badly underestimated, was that Britain was producing more planes than Germany. It was easier for the British to replace planes that were shot down. If the number of Royal air Force (RAF) and German planes shot down was roughly equal, Britain would win the battle.

In addition, when RAF planes were shot down, the pilots might parachute to safety and be flying again the next day. German pilots who parachuted or crash-landed came down in England and were taken prisoner—or in the English Channel, where they were likely to drown.

This last advantage was particularly important because it helped make up for Britain's one great disadvantage: a shortage of trained fighter pilots. Fighter pilots take a long time to train, and Germany started with many more experienced airmen. During the worst days of the Battle of Britain, the RAF sometimes had more planes ready to fly than they had pilots to fly them.

The Luftwaffe now shifted to attacks on factories and military installations throughout England. Although they heavily damaged their targets, the Luftwaffe lost too many planes to continue.

Then the Germans changed their focus again. Instead of attacking targets all over England, the Luftwaffe concentrated all its power against the RAF's airfields and nearby ground-control stations. From late August to September 7, they knocked out some of the RAF's bases and destroyed nearly 300 British fighters. It they had continued, they could have crippled the RAF.

But they decided to shift their main target once more, giving the RAF time to repair its damaged airfields. Part of the reason was that winter was coming and the weather over the Channel would soon turn stormy. A German invasion of Britain would have to come soon or be postponed until at least the following spring. Hitler decided to send bombers against London, Britain's great capital, with a population of 7 million people. The purpose was to destroy the British people's will to fight by terrorizing them and to force the RAF into a massive battle.

Beginning on September 7, large formations of German bombers, with escorts of fighter planes, attacked London, raining bombs on the docks along the Thames River and other military targets, but also blasting homes, schools, and hospitals. The fighters of the RAF tried to shoot them down before they reached London, and the 2,000 antiaircraft guns of the heavily defended city blasted them when they arrived. The largest raid, on September 15, included 200 bombers. Every

Royal Air Force Spitfire fighter planes patrolling the English coast. *(Reproduced by permission of the Corbis Corporation [Bellevue])*

These children sit in front of their house in London, which has been bombed by the German Luftwaffe. *(Reproduced by permission of the National Archives and Records Administration)*

RAF fighter within flying range was in the air, and 60 German bombers were shot down.

These attacks on London continued until the end of the month, but by September 17, Hitler had decided to "postpone" the German invasion of Britain. He would never schedule it again. The pilots of the RAF had saved Britain. Churchill said of them that never before "has so much been owed by so many to so few."

The "Blitz"

Despite their lack of success against the RAF, the Luftwaffe actually increased its attempts to terrorize the British people. Throughout October and November, the Germans shifted to nighttime raids over London. (All the previous action in the Battle of Britain had been during the day.) Night bombing was completely inaccurate at that time, so this was

not really an attempt to hit military targets or factories. It was meant to cause as much damage and loss of life as possible.

This is the period that the people of England called "the Blitz." Although sirens warned them of the nightly attacks and they hid in cellars and underground shelters—including subway stations—40,000 Londoners died in the air raids. Large parts of London and other cities were destroyed. To protect

Germany's nighttime raids over London were not aimed at military targets but were meant to terrorize the civilian population.
(Reproduced by permission of Corbis-Bettman)

them from the bombing, parents sent thousands of children from their homes in the big cities to live with strangers in the countryside who had volunteered to take them in. (Children's experiences during the war are discussed in Chapter 8.)

But the German armed forces had been defeated for the first time. Britain, although alone, was still fighting.

The War Expands

3

From the time that France surrendered in June 1940 until Germany invaded the Soviet Union (Russia) almost exactly a year later, Great Britain was the only major country fighting Nazi Germany and its main ally, Italy. Yet this period saw the war expand into new areas and draw in more countries.

Help for Britain

Even in the summer of 1940, Britain was not completely alone. Four distant countries that had once been British colonies and still had close ties to Britain also declared war on Germany: Canada, Australia, New Zealand, and South Africa. They sent tens of thousands of soldiers, who fought in their own units throughout the war, as well as money, food, and industrial products. In addition, troops from British colonies, especially India, played a major role in several areas of fighting. "British" troops often included large numbers of units from these other countries.

Some of Britain's most important help, however, came from a country that was still neutral in the war—the United

Troops from countries that were once British colonies, like Canada and Australia, as well as troops from countries still ruled by Britain, like these Indian soldiers fighting in Italy in 1943, often played a major role in the war. *(Reproduced by permission of AP/Wide World Photos)*

States. A neutral country supposedly does not take sides in a war. But most Americans favored the Allies (Britain, France, and the countries that joined them against Germany) from the beginning of the war. After France's defeat, when it looked as if Germany would win, pro-British feelings became even stronger. In the autumn of 1940, a public opinion poll found that 75 percent of the American people wanted to help Britain. At the same time, however, 83 percent said they did not want the United States to enter the war.

Isolationism

The traditional American attitude, from the time of the founding of the country, was that the United States should stay out of Europe's quarrels. In 1917, the United States had joined Britain and France against Germany in World War I, but many Americans came to believe this had been a mistake. They felt that thousands of Americans had died, and millions of dollars had been spent and Europe still had the same problems. They thought that America, protected by two great oceans, should remain safely isolated from Europe's troubles.

These ideas, usually called isolationism, were very powerful during the 1920s and the early 1930s. Adolf Hitler's rise in Germany altered American public opinion, however. The Nazis' brutal methods, their banning of all other political parties, and their destruction of labor unions had disturbed many Americans. The Nazi campaign against the Jews horrified people all over the world. (The early years of the Nazi government are described in Chapter 1.) And as Nazism and similar political systems came to power and destroyed democracy in one European country after another, more Americans began to feel that these events threatened their own freedom.

But isolationism remained an important political force in the country. The isolationist "America First" organization, founded in September 1940, had 850,000 members. Isolationists included respected figures like Charles Lindbergh, who was a national hero for being the first person to fly by himself, nonstop, across the Atlantic. Although some isolationists admired Nazi Germany and opposed American involvement for this reason, pro-Nazi sentiments were never a major force in the United States.

Increasing American involvement

President Franklin D. Roosevelt understood, and probably agreed with, the American people's conflicting desires: he made it clear that American policy would be to help the Allies while staying out of the war. He called the United States "the Arsenal of Democracy," meaning that American industrial power would provide arms—but not troops—for the Allies. After France surrendered, Britain's need for American help became more urgent.

Britain depended on imports more than almost any other country. Besides having no petroleum or rubber and few metals besides iron, Britain grew only half the food its people needed. American wheat, meat, and other food, shipped across the Atlantic, were as important as tanks and cannons. By 1941, almost 30 percent of Britain's food came from the United States.

As Nazism and similar political systems came to power and destroyed democracy in one European country after another, more Americans began to feel that these events threatened their own freedom.

Did President Roosevelt Want War?

There has been much debate over the motives behind some of President Franklin D. Roosevelt's decisions regarding U.S. involvement in World War II prior to the country's formally entering the war. Many of his opponents—and even some of his supporters—believed that he secretly wanted the United States to go to war against Germany. However, Roosevelt knew that the American people and Congress would oppose American involvement. Therefore, some people claim, he did everything possible to make Germany attack the United States. For example, in the spring of 1941, he ordered the American navy to protect British ships. In September 1941, three months before the United States officially entered the war, he ordered American warships to fire on any German submarine seen in what the United States considered its "Atlantic Security Zone." If American ships were sunk and American sailors killed, the American people would be much more willing to declare war on Germany.

Other historians point to evidence, including conversations that were not made public at the time, that Roosevelt meant exactly what he said. He would do everything possible—including *risking* war with Germany—to prevent the Nazis from winning. Roosevelt thought, however, that he would still be able to keep the country out of war. Indeed, he did not ask Congress to declare war when German submarines did sink American warships while the United States was still neutral.

Regardless of Roosevelt's intensions, the United States finally entered the war only after Japan bombed Pearl Harbor in Hawaii on December 7, 1941. Even then, the United States did not declare war on Germany: it was Germany, a few days after the Japanese attack, that declared war on the United States.

But American help went far beyond food. In September 1940, the United States gave Britain fifty outdated American destroyers, warships often used to escort merchant ships (civilian ships carrying freight) and defend them against enemy attacks. In return, Britain gave the United States the right to station American naval bases on various British islands near the United States.

The American destroyers, though old, were very useful to Britain. However, the British got something even more important from the agreement: by providing naval bases, the agreement meant that the United States could take over the defense of areas that the British, with their navy fighting all over the world, could not defend against German attack.

In addition, the agreement helped connect the British and American defense efforts in the minds of many Americans. The same was true of an agreement between the United States and Canada on a common plan to defend North America from possible attack. Since Canada was at war with Germany, this meant that the United States was committing itself to side with Canada (and Britain) if Germany tried to carry the war across the Atlantic.

In the summer of 1940, Congress voted to increase the budget for construction of American warships. These new ships would double the size of the U.S. Navy. In September, the United States began drafting men into the army, the first time this had been done while the country was not at war. The small peacetime American army would be greatly enlarged and equipped with modern weapons.

American involvement continued to increase. In March 1941, Congress passed the Lend-Lease agreement. Although the terms were complicated, Lend-Lease really meant that Britain could buy American goods—including weapons—on credit and pay back the money after the war. This was extremely important because the cost of the war had used up almost all of Britain's money. Within weeks, Congress voted $7 billion as the first installment for Lend-Lease, an enormous amount at the time. Everyone understood that Britain would never be able to pay back its debt if it lost the war. In effect, America was betting billions of dollars on a British victory. (The law did not specifically name the countries that were to benefit, which allowed Roosevelt to extend Lend-Lease to other countries later. Within a year, Lend-Lease aid was flowing in great quantities to the Soviet Union.)

Only a few weeks after Congress passed the Lend-Lease law, Roosevelt expanded the "American Security Zone" to cover much of the Atlantic Ocean. Within the zone, the U.S. Navy would protect American merchant ships, including those carrying weapons for Britain, and would report the presence of all German ships to the British navy. By May, American warships were escorting convoys (large groups of ships sailing together for protection) of American ships all the way to Britain. Beginning in June 1941, British merchant ships were

Lend-Lease really meant that Britain could buy American goods— including weapons—on credit and pay back the money after the war.

Perhaps the most important factor in the Battle of the Atlantic was American industry's ability to produce more ships than anyone had imagined possible.

allowed to sail in American convoys, which meant they would be protected by the U.S. Navy.

In April, the United States had signed an agreement with the Danish ambassador in Washington, D.C., that called for the two countries to defend the giant island of Greenland, a Danish possession off the northeast coast of Canada. Since Denmark was under military occupation by Germany, this really meant that the United States would defend Greenland if the Germans tried to use it as a base to attack British ships. Soon afterward, a unit of United States Marines replaced British forces in Iceland, an island country in the North Atlantic, for the same purpose.

The Battle of the Atlantic

These measures were part of the "Battle of the Atlantic." As vital food and weapons sailed east to Britain, German submarines lay in wait. The German navy relied on submarines because it had relatively few surface warships and the powerful British navy hunted down and sank most of them. In the last eight months of 1941, the submarines, known as U-boats (because the German word for "submarine" begins with a "u"), sank 328 British merchant ships. This was about one and a half times the number of ships that Britain could build in a year.

If the U-boats had continued at this rate, they would have won the Battle of the Atlantic, and the British people would have starved. The British and Canadian navies (and, increasingly, the American navy) took measures to protect the ships. The U-boats responded with countermeasures. The convoy system was one example on the Allied side. On the German side, the U-boats used a new tactic of attacking in large groups, which were known as wolf packs. The advantage shifted back and forth as both sides added technical improvements. For example, each side temporarily had the upper hand when it was able to intercept and decode the radio messages of the other.

Perhaps the most important factor in the battle was American industry's ability to produce more ships than anyone had imagined possible. These included a standard freighter, called the Liberty ship, which took an average of only three months to build. In October 1942, three completed Liberty ships left American shipyards every *day*. So even when the

Rows of Liberty ships in
a California shipyard.
*(Reproduced by permission of
the National Archives and
Records Administration)*

U-boats sank dozens of Allied freighters in a month, the number of ships successfully crossing to Britain continued to rise.

The submarines had a strategic edge when they
attacked underwater. They could fire their deadly torpedoes
from beneath the sea. The warships protecting the convoys
had electronic devices to find submarines, but they could not
measure how deep the U-boats were. So the underwater bombs

A surfaced German U-boat sinking after a combined attack by several aircraft.
(Reproduced by permission of the Corbis Corporation [Bellevue])

that the warships dropped overboard (called depth charges) often exploded too far above or below the U-boat to cause serious damage.

But submarines of that time had to spend much of their time on the surface in order to recharge their batteries. They were in great danger if caught there by airplanes. Because of this, the U-boats usually surfaced at night, but the British (and the Americans after the United States entered the war) used radar and improved searchlights on long-range bombers to find and destroy more and more U-boats. As American production of these bombers increased, the U-boats began to lose the battle. By May 1943, Germany was losing submarines twice as fast as it could build new ones. Faced with these losses, the German navy stopped sending U-boats into the Atlantic.

Almost 2,500 Allied merchant ships and 175 warships sank during the Battle of the Atlantic. But almost 700 out of 830 U-boats were destroyed. Out of 40,000 men in the German crews, more than 25,000 were killed and another 5,000 taken prisoner after their submarines were destroyed.

The war in the desert

While the U-boats tried to strangle British sea supplies, other battles were being fought on land. In North Africa, Libya had been a colony of Italy, Germany's most important ally, since 1912, and 200,000 Italian soldiers were stationed there. In September 1940, Italian dictator Benito Mussolini ordered this army to cross the border eastward into British-controlled Egypt. Although the Italians stopped after only 60 miles and prepared defensive positions, the invasion greatly worried the British. A successful Italian invasion of Egypt would threaten the Suez Canal in the northeast region of the country. Without the canal, ships going from the Indian Ocean to the Mediterranean—and then to Britain—would have to travel all the way around Africa, which takes much longer and uses much more fuel. Even more important, beyond Egypt are the oil fields of Iraq and Arabia. The Axis powers (the countries fighting on the German side) had few safe supplies of oil (Libyan oil had not yet been discovered), and this was one of their greatest weaknesses.

In December 1940, the greatly outnumbered British surprised the Italians by attacking. The Italians retreated, chased by the British for 400 miles into Libya. By the time the retreat ended in February 1941, the British had captured 130,000 Italian troops.

The fighting, like all the later battles, was along a narrow strip of land with only one real road that lay between the

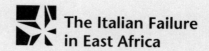

The Italian Failure in East Africa

In August 1940, an Italian army captured the undefended British colony of Somaliland (part of today's Somalia). The Italians already controlled part of Somaliland as a colony and Ethiopia, which they had invaded and conquered in 1935. It looked as if Italian dictator Benito Mussolini's dream of an African empire for Italy was coming true.

But the Italian success did not last long. In February 1941, a British force consisting mostly of Indian troops moved south from Sudan. Another force, mainly South Africans but also including Kenyans and Nigerians, moved north from Kenya. (Britain controlled Sudan, Kenya, and far-off Nigeria.) A third group, landing from the sea, recaptured British Somaliland. The Allied forces quickly captured Italian Somaliland and moved into Ethiopia. At the same time, large numbers of Ethiopians who opposed Italy began a campaign of guerrilla warfare. Although there was some heavy fighting, the Italians were poorly equipped and had no way to get supplies from home. By May, the entire Italian army in East Africa, more than 70,000 men, had surrendered.

General Erwin Rommel, "the Desert Fox," in North Africa.
(Reproduced by permission of the National Archives and Records Administration)

Mediterranean Sea to the north and the almost impassable desert to the south. Supplies and reinforcements for both armies had to come by sea. Each time one of the armies was successful, it moved farther away from the ports where its supplies arrived. The army that retreated was closer to its sources of resupply. So each success increased the danger that the other side would be able to launch a successful counterattack. And that is exactly what happened from December 1940 until October 1942.

The Afrika korps

Although Mussolini was reluctant to admit that he needed help after the Italian army's disaster, he agreed to allow a German force to land in Libya in a bid to save the situation. Its commander was General Erwin Rommel, one of the most successful of the German Panzer (tank) commanders during

the conquest of France. Although the main part of his force was Italian, Rommel's German troops were known as the Afrika korps. They would soon become popular heroes in Germany. Rommel, "the Desert Fox," became the most admired German general at home and the one most feared by the Allies.

In March 1941, Rommel attacked the British and within a few weeks forced them all the way back to where they

A successful Italian invasion of Egypt threatened the Suez Canal, an important shortcut for British ships traveling to the Indian Ocean.

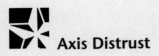

Axis Distrust

Italy's decision to invade Greece without telling Germany was not unusual for the Axis partners. The Italian leadership, including Benito Mussolini, was worried that Germany was beginning to treat Italy like one of the countries it had conquered rather than as an ally. And the Germans rarely told the Italians what they were planning either. The German generals had a very low opinion of the Italian army, which they did not hide.

It is true that Italian troops had a poor record in the war. But the Italian army was almost always poorly equipped and usually badly led. The soldiers had little confidence in their military leaders. For this reason, a minor setback could easily cause the troops to lose their willingness to fight—and turn a battle into a major defeat. In addition, more and more Italians—including soldiers—came to oppose Italy's participation in the war, which seemed to be entirely for Germany's benefit. As more Italians died or were captured, Mussolini's popularity faded.

The lack of joint planning among the Axis powers (later including Japan) differed from the close cooperation that developed between the British and Americans.

had been in December. A British counterattack failed, but a second major British assault, in November, forced the Germans and Italians back to where *Rommel* had started. In January 1942, it was Rommel's turn again, and again the British retreated into Egypt. In each of these attacks, retreats, and counterattacks, each side lost fuel, tanks, planes, and—of course—soldiers.

Despite the repeated advances and retreats, the desert war remained a standoff, almost as if both sides had simply stood still. The deadlock was not broken until Rommel was forced to fight the British to his east and an invading American army to his west. (These events are described in Chapter 10.)

Italy attacks in Europe

Even before his African schemes ended in disaster, Mussolini was turning his attention to Europe. He wanted Italy to return to the glory of the ancient Roman Empire. Most historians also think that jealousy of his ally, Hitler, played a major part in his decisions.

In April 1939, before the beginning of the war, Italy had sent an army to take over Albania, a small, poor country across the Adriatic Sea from Italy. Mussolini decided to use his base in Albania to invade and conquer Greece, and Italian troops attacked on October 28. Mussolini apparently ordered the invasion of Greece without informing the Germans. If he had, they would probably have pressured him to give up the idea. Hitler was anxious to avoid any military actions in Europe that might interfere with his secret plan to invade the Soviet Union, which was scheduled for the following spring.

The Italian army, despite vastly outnumbering the Greeks, was—as usual—poorly equipped, and the invasion began without sufficient planning. After some early successes, the Italian offensive stalled. In the middle of November, the Greek army counterattacked, quickly drove the Italians back into Albania, and crossed the border in pursuit. By January 1941, the Italians were in danger of being forced to evacuate Albania.

Germany moves south

Just as in Africa, Mussolini had to ask Germany for help. The Italian defeat in Greece set off a complicated chain reaction, as one country after another in the region was impacted. The Greeks had asked for British help, and Britain sent them troops from North Africa. The British forces in Greece would eventually number 68,000 men.

Hitler had not wanted to do anything that might delay the invasion of the Soviet Union. But Italy's attack on Greece had once again brought British troops to Europe. The Germans did not want a threat to their south while they fought in Russia. Among other dangers, British planes taking off from Greece could bomb the oil fields in Romania, the main source of petroleum for Germany. In addition, Hitler felt he needed to help Mussolini because the Italian defeat might encourage other countries to resist the Axis.

But moving German troops to Greece meant going through other countries. After much German pressure, Bulgaria, which borders Greece, signed an alliance with Germany in March 1941 agreeing to allow German troops to invade Greece from Bulgarian territory.

Germany also wanted to attack Greece through Yugoslavia. On March 25, Prince Paul, the regent of Yugoslavia, agreed to join the Axis. (A regent is someone who rules in place of a king or queen, for example, when the king is too young, as was the case in Yugoslavia.) Two days later, a group of Yugoslav army officers who opposed the alliance with Germany overthrew Prince Paul and withdrew the agreement.

The Italian defeat in Greece set off a complicated chain reaction, as one country after another in the region was impacted.

A German antiaircraft
gun on the lower slopes
of the Acropolis in Athens,
with the ancient Greek
temple the Parthenon seen
in the background.
*(Reproduced by permission of
AP/Wide World Photos)*

They were encouraged to do this by British (and probably
American) secret agents.

An enraged Hitler ordered the German army to change
its plans. Since Yugoslavia would not allow German troops
through to invade Greece, they would attack Yugoslavia too.
The Germans invaded both countries on April 6.

Although the Yugoslav army had a million soldiers, the
Germans easily broke through. The Luftwaffe (the German air
force) heavily bombed the Yugoslav capital of Belgrade and
other targets. The Germans entered the city on April 12, and
Yugoslavia surrendered on April 17. Only 151 German soldiers
were killed in the invasion.

The victors now dismantled the country. Germany,
Italy, Hungary, and Bulgaria all took parts of Yugoslav territory.
Serbia, one of the main areas of Yugoslavia, was put under Ger-
man military administration. A new "independent" country of
Croatia was created in western Yugoslavia, ruled by a pro-Nazi

June, 1942

- Axis Powers
- Allied with Axis
- Occupied by Axis
- Neutral

government that was violently anti-Serb. Although victory had been incredibly easy, the Germans would face much greater resistance in Yugoslavia in the following years. (Later events in Yugoslavia are described at the end of Chapter 6.)

The German invasion of Greece, starting from Bulgaria, was almost as easy. The Greek army was still concentrated against the Italians in Albania, and the British force was not large enough to stop the Germans. The Germans entered Athens, the

Countries allied with the Axis powers, countries occupied by the Axis powers, and neutral countries, in June 1942.

Greek capital, on April 27. The British were forced to evacuate their troops by sea—leaving most of their equipment behind.

Many British troops relocated to the large Greek island of Crete in the Mediterranean Sea. A few weeks later, German parachute troops landed on the island and, with strong Luftwaffe support, defeated the British and Greek defenders, who heavily outnumbered them. Once again, the British evacuated some of their troops by sea, but Germany's spectacular victory was a cause of great gloom in Britain.

These events were a terrible reminder that less than a year after it had evacuated its troops from France, Britain was not strong enough to maintain a foothold in Europe. Germany, Italy, and their Axis partners now controlled almost the whole continent, up to the border of Soviet Russia. Beyond that border, however, lay the land that Hitler had always wanted.

Land, anticommunism, and racism

Hitler had always wanted to conquer vast new territory. According to him, Germany needed it for *Lebensraum,* or "room to live." This word implied that without this room, Germany could not survive. Germany was supposedly too small for its population.

Hitler believed that this new land would come from eastern Europe. Germany would conquer White Russia (now the country of Belarus) and Ukraine. Both had long been part of the Russian Empire. Now they were the western part of the Soviet Union (short for the Union of Soviet Socialist Republics, or USSR), the country that the Communists had set up after overthrowing the Russian Empire. In addition, the eastern half of Poland had become part of the Soviet Union in 1939. This was part of a deal Hitler made with the Soviet government just before Germany invaded Poland on September 1, 1939, and conquered the western half of the country. (This deal, known as the Nazi-Soviet Pact, is described in Chapter 2.) The Soviets had also taken over the three small countries of Lithuania, Latvia, and Estonia on the shores of the Baltic Sea.

Since all these areas were now part of the communist-controlled Soviet Union, going to war against the Soviets would satisfy both Hitler's hatred of communists and his desire to conquer territory. In addition, like everything else in Hitler's mind, these goals were mixed up with Nazi ideas about "race," a word they used in a completely unscientific sense. The Nazis believed that Germans were a superior race that had the right to rule over the "inferior" people of eastern Europe. Germany would take over the land and populate it with Germans. The Poles, Russians, Ukrainians, White Russians, and others would be used as sources of cheap labor.

For Hitler and the Nazis, the invasion of the Soviet Union would be a war to conquer land for the "superior" German race, to destroy communism, and to destroy the Jews.

The western Soviet Union, including eastern Poland, was also home to 5 million Jews. According to Nazi racial theories, the Jews were not even people—they were "subhumans." In Hitler's mind the Communist government of the Soviet Union was part of a Jewish plot to rule the world. Jews and communists were the same thing to the Nazis. For Hitler and the Nazis, the invasion of the Soviet Union would be a war to conquer land for the "superior" German race, to destroy communism, and to destroy the Jews. (The Nazis' actions against the Jews of the Soviet Union are described in Chapter 7.)

It was this combination of motives that made the German invasion of the Soviet Union so murderous. The destruction and cruelty went far beyond even the "normal" horror of modern war.

The invasion

On June 22, 1941, Germany launched its surprise attack on the Soviet Union. It was code-named Operation Barbarossa (which means "Red Beard"), the nickname of a German emperor of the Middle Ages. The Soviet army and government were completely unprepared. The German forces, led by tanks, pushed into Soviet territory with tremendous speed. Often, whole Soviet divisions, even whole armies, were trapped behind the advancing German Panzer divisions. (A division is a large unit of an army, usually about 15,000 men, though Soviet divisions were often smaller.) Then the German infantry, moving much more slowly than the tanks, would destroy these "pockets" of surrounded Soviet troops. Although the trapped Soviet soldiers usually fought fiercely, tens of thousands surrendered when they ran out of food and ammunition. The rest of the Soviet army retreated toward the east, trying to prevent a total collapse. The German air force

Armored half-tracks, part of a Panzer group, and German troops move deep into Russia, summer 1941. *(Reproduced by permission of AP/Wide World Photos)*

attacked the roads, railroads, cities, and towns. The German blitzkrieg (lightning war) caused chaos and panic, just as it had in Poland and France. (The German military tactics known as blitzkrieg are described in Chapter 2.)

After less than three weeks, the Germans, joined by Hungarian, Romanian, and Italian units, had advanced 280 miles and taken 300,000 prisoners. Fifteen hundred Soviet tanks, 2,000 planes, and 3,000 cannons had been destroyed or captured.

These totals kept growing as the Germans continued to advance. In September, in a great battle around Kiev, the capital of Ukraine, the Germans trapped 50 Soviet divisions. Pounded by the Luftwaffe and attacked by Panzers and German infantry, more than 650,000 Soviet troops were taken prisoner in this one battle. By now, the Germans had captured almost 3 million Russian soldiers.

In the first months of the Soviet invasion, the Germans were even more successful than they had been in Poland

Poland and western Soviet Union, 1939–41. Shaded areas show German-occupied Poland and areas of Poland taken by the Soviet Union. The arrows indicate the direction of Germany's invading armies.

and France. But there was a big difference. Although the Germans gained hundreds of miles of territory, there was still room for the Soviets to retreat. Although millions of Soviet soldiers had been killed or captured, there were still millions more fighting or ready for battle. The Germans had destroyed thousands of tanks, cannons, and planes and captured many of the factories where they were built. But there were more factories the Germans hadn't reached, and the Soviets were transferring whole factories and building new ones in the east, far from the reach of the Germans. By the end of August 1941, the Soviets had moved more than 1,500 factories east by railroad. Many more would follow in the next months.

The great spaces of Russia, the large population that could provide men to replace the lost armies, and the vast industrial potential of the country meant that the German invasion, though astounding in military terms, was not enough to defeat the Soviet Union. After the first few weeks of confusion,

A German soldier rides past a burning Russian tank during Germany's invasion of Russia, 1941.
(Reproduced by permission of AP/Wide World Photos)

the Soviet army had fought hard, and although it continued to take heavy losses, it also inflicted heavy losses on the Germans.

As they retreated, the Russians tried to destroy every bridge and railroad line, every dam on every river, every warehouse and barn—leaving as little as possible for the invaders to use. The Germans often found nothing left but "scorched earth."

The three invading German Army Groups were spread over a battlefront hundreds of miles wide from north to south. As they advanced eastward, the front kept growing, like a fan being spread out. Every mile that they advanced east was another mile to send supplies over the primitive Russian road system. Very few roads were paved, and the dirt roads turned to mud whenever it rained. Although tracked vehicles, like tanks, could sometimes travel over these roads and through the fields, wheeled vehicles had to wait until the roads dried out. The tanks were delayed, waiting for food, ammunition, and—most important—fuel to arrive in trucks or horse-drawn wagons.

Two symbols

By August 30, Army Group North reached the city of Leningrad, the second-largest Soviet city, with 3 million people. Leningrad also had great symbolic importance. It had been the capital of Imperial Russia before the Communist revolution, when it was called Saint Petersburg. Then it was renamed in honor of Vladimir Lenin, the founder of the Communist government. (Today, the city is again called Saint Petersburg.) German troops nearly surrounded the city. The only way that the Russians could bring supplies into Leningrad was across Lake Ladoga, a huge lake northeast of the city. The people remaining in the city dug almost 400 miles of antitank ditches and built thousands of blockhouses to stop the Germans. Under its new commander, Marshal Georgy Zhukov, the Soviet army made a stand and stopped the German advance.

For the next two and a half years, the people of Leningrad lived under the German guns and bombs. The few supplies they received had to be brought 125 miles through deep arctic forests and then across Lake Ladoga in boats; in the winter, trucks crossed the frozen water. Death from starvation and freezing became common. Fifty thousand people died in the city in December 1941. By the time the Germans were finally driven away in the spring of 1944, 1 million citizens of Leningrad had died. The Germans never captured the city.

Meanwhile, Army Group Center continued driving east toward Moscow. Moscow was the Soviet capital, headquarters and symbol of the world communist movement. Supposedly, the leading German troops were so close they could see the reflection of the sun off the golden domes of the churches in the Kremlin, the ancient walled district that housed the Soviet government.

Again, as in Leningrad, the civilian population dug trenches; again the Soviet army made a stand. As the autumn rains turned the roads and fields into sticky mud that even tanks could not cross, the German advance halted. When the rains turned into snow and the tanks could again cross the now-frozen ground, it was the Russians who attacked.

By the time the Germans were finally driven away in the spring of 1944, 1 million citizens of Leningrad had died. The Germans never captured the city.

"General Winter"

The German troops were not fitted with winter gear. This was partly because giving them winter clothes and special boots would mean admitting that the war would be long. The German leaders feared that this would discourage the troops and hurt their ability to fight. As a result, thousands of German soldiers developed frostbitten feet and were unable to walk. The engines of the German tanks and trucks would not work; the gasoline froze; rubber tires turned as hard as metal. The horses, hungry and cold like the men, were too weak to pull artillery through the deep snowdrifts.

Every German officer—and every Soviet one as well—knew the story of how the French general and emperor Napoleon had led a great army to Moscow in 1812, winning battle after battle. The Russians had burned everything as they retreated, leaving nothing for the invaders to eat. Then the Russian winter and the Russian soldiers together had destroyed their seemingly unbeatable enemy.

Now, more than a century later, the same thing seemed to be happening to Hitler's army. As the temperature kept dropping (at times it reached 40 degrees below zero), with howling winds and blowing snow, the Soviet counteroffensive—commanded by Marshal Zhukov—forced the Germans back from Moscow. At times, it looked as if much of Army Group Center might be surrounded and destroyed. For the first time, signs of panic appeared among some German soldiers.

But the German generals saved most of their forces by retreating and forming defensive positions, and waiting for spring. They were back where they had been in October—but still deep inside Russia. The German army had suffered a defeat—its first major defeat of the war—but it was not yet beaten. The German soldiers had experienced the power of "General Winter" and the way the Russian soldiers could fight in defense of their country. But hundreds of thousands more Russian and German soldiers would die before, like Napoleon, the defeated Germans would leave Russia forever.

Japan Attacks and America Goes to War

4

The war in Europe soon affected Asia. Although it was not part of the European war, Japan was an ally of Nazi Germany and Italy. The three countries had signed an agreement in 1936, called the Anti-Comintern Treaty. (The "Comintern" was the "Communist International," the organization of world Communist parties run by the Soviet Union. Germany, Japan, and Italy used this name to make their alliance sound like a defensive agreement against communism.) The governments of the three countries were similar in many ways. Each was antidemocratic, each glorified military strength, and each wanted to conquer new territory.

By 1940, the Japanese government was largely dominated by militarists, extremists in the army and navy and their supporters who wanted the armed forces to control Japan and organize Japanese society along military principles. They believed Japan had a sacred mission to conquer new territory to provide the natural resources that Japan lacked.

Japan had been expanding its empire in Asia throughout the 1930s. It had been brutally fighting a war against China since 1937. The Japanese had conquered the great cities

Areas of eastern Asia under Japanese control in 1941.

on China's coast as well as other areas, but a complete victory proved more difficult than Japan had expected. Although Japan had one million soldiers in China, the Chinese armies were protected by the mountainous geography of China's interior. For several years the war was deadlocked. (These events are described in more detail in Chapter 1.)

The Japanese government believed it could finally defeat China by preventing the Chinese from receiving military supplies from the rest of the world, including France, Britain, and especially the United States. The Chinese armies, cut off from ports, had only a few supply routes. One was the Burma Road, a motorway that cut through the high mountains of Burma (present-day Myanmar), a British colony. But the most important was a railroad that ran to China from northern Vietnam, which was then a part of the French colony of Indochina. (French Indochina also included what are now the smaller countries of Laos and Cambodia.)

The events in Europe in the spring of 1940 gave Japan a chance to close these routes. After France surrendered to Germany in June, the Germans allowed a French government to remain in power in the southern part of the country. This government, known as Vichy (the town where the government was based), still controlled most French colonies overseas. Japan demanded the right to station troops and establish airfields in northern Vietnam. After Japanese troops in the area briefly attacked the French in September 1940, Vichy agreed to the Japanese demands.

Japan also demanded that Britain close the Burma Road. At that time, Britain was threatened by a German invasion and could not risk another war with Japan. In July 1940, Britain agreed to close the Burma Road for three months.

Japan's new goals

The German victories in Europe may have aided Japan's attempts to conquer China, but they also opened much greater opportunities for Japan: it was now impossible for France and very difficult for Britain to defend their vast colonial empires in Asia.

Germany had also conquered and occupied the Netherlands (often called Holland; in English the people are usually called Dutch). The Dutch government had fled to Britain, where it established a government-in-exile, considered the rightful government of the Netherlands by the Allies, the countries fighting Germany. This government controlled the Dutch East Indies (today's Indonesia), a large group of islands between Southeast Asia and Australia. Indonesia had oil—the most important resource for a modern war, and one that Japan lacked entirely. The Dutch and Indonesian troops stationed in the Dutch East Indies could not expect help from the Dutch government-in-exile if Japan attacked the islands.

Taking over the British, French, and Dutch colonies in Asia would give Japan a huge new empire with large quantities of oil, rubber, and important metals such as tin. And Japanese companies could sell their products in this empire without competition from other countries. By the fall of 1940, the Japanese government had decided to invade these areas. Japanese mili-

Japanese, German, and Italian officials signing the Tripartite Pact, September 1940. *(Reproduced by permission of AP/Wide World Photos)*

tary leaders were confident they could defeat the British and Dutch colonial armies and navies. France was not even a threat because of Germany's domination of the Vichy government.

The only other major power in the Pacific was the United States. American aid to China was already a major concern to Japan, and Japanese expansion in Southeast Asia and the Dutch East Indies would threaten the Philippines. The Philippines were controlled by the United States, which had seized the islands from Spain during the Spanish-American War in 1898. The islands were scheduled to become independent in 1944, and the last American troops were supposed to leave two years later, but in the meantime the Philippines were like an American colony. Even apart from the issue of the Philippines, Japan knew that the United States would not accept total Japanese control of Southeast Asia and the western Pacific. That would shut the United States out of economically important areas and might lead to even more Japanese expansion in the future.

By the summer of 1940, some Japanese leaders were convinced that their plan of conquest would require war with the United States. And they believed that the sooner the war began, the more likely Japan was to win. The United States had begun a major program of building warships. The longer Japan waited, the stronger the American navy would become. And there would never be a better time to fight against preoccupied Britain and the occupied Netherlands.

In September 1940, Japan, Germany, and Italy signed a new agreement, known as the Tripartite Pact, which means "three-party treaty." From Japan's point of view, the treaty guaranteed German support for its plans in Asia and the Pacific. In this sense, the treaty was really aimed at the American government. It was a warning that if the United States tried to stop Japan, it might have to go to war against Germany and Italy too.

A few months later, Japan took another important step in preparing for war. Japanese conquests in northern China had brought them into conflict with the Soviet Union. In 1939, Soviet and Japanese troops had fought vicious border battles there, and the Soviet army had inflicted heavy losses on the Japanese, much to Japan's surprise. (The unexpected strength of the Soviet army was another reason for Japan to attack in the Pacific—away from Russia.) In April 1941, Japan signed a treaty with the Soviets, in which each country promised that it would remain neutral if the other went to war. Japan would be able to expand southward without worrying about the Soviet Union to the north. When Germany invaded the Soviet Union in June, the danger that the Soviet army might interfere with the Japanese in China became even less likely. (The German attack on the Soviet Union is described in Chapter 3.)

The Tripartite Pact meant that if the United States tried to stop Japan, it might have to go to war against Germany and Italy too.

Tensions between Japan and the United States

In May 1941, the United States extended its "Lend-Lease" program to China. In effect, this meant that China could buy arms and supplies from the United States on long-term credit. By doing this, the United States was confirming that it would continue to support China in its war against Japan.

General Hideki Tojo, who was already minister of war (in charge of the army), also became the prime minister (head of the government) of Japan in October 1941.
(Reproduced by permission of The Library of Congress)

At the same time, talks between Japan and the United States began in Washington, D.C.; they continued for months. Most historians agree that the negotiations never had any chance of success because each side insisted on points to which the other would never agree. The Americans wanted to prevent Japan from controlling China and Southeast Asia. To the Japanese, that meant remaining at the economic mercy of other countries. The United States, Britain, and the other Western powers would never accept such a situation for themselves. The Japanese felt insulted and threatened by what they viewed as an American attempt to treat Japan as a second-rate power.

While the negotiations continued, the situation in Asia worsened. On July 24, Vichy France agreed to allow Japanese troops into southern Indochina. Unlike Japan's earlier demands, this didn't seem to have anything to do with the war with China. Instead, it seemed to the United States—and to Britain and the Netherlands, too—that Japan was planning to move against Indonesia, British Malaya, and perhaps the Philippines.

The United States demanded that Japan withdraw from Indochina and two days later froze all Japanese assets in the United States. In effect, this meant that Japan could not buy any goods from the United States. Most important, America cut off all oil shipments. Britain and the Dutch government-in-exile also banned the export of oil to Japan, which now had almost no sources of petroleum. It also faced serious shortages of other products. Japan had expected the American petroleum embargo (a government ban on trade) and had stockpiled large quantities of oil. It had enough to last three years in normal circumstances, or about eighteen months in wartime, when tanks, trucks, and planes use immense amounts of fuel. But the Japanese army estimated that it would take three years to win the war in China. This was another reason for Japan to either settle its differences with the United States or go to war—soon. In October 1941, the Japanese government finally decided to go to war with the United States.

Pearl Harbor

On November 26, 1941, a great Japanese fleet began a 2,800-mile voyage across the Pacific. It included four battleships, two heavy cruisers, ten destroyers, and two dozen long-range submarines. All of these warships had a single purpose: to protect the six large aircraft carriers in the fleet. On the carriers were 360 planes, including dive-bombers and planes that were equipped to drop torpedoes designed to operate in shallow water.

A courier had delivered the orders for the operation so that no one could intercept radio messages from naval headquarters to the various officers. The Japanese fleet kept absolute radio silence throughout its long voyage at sea. The ships started in the northern Pacific, far from the usual routes of commercial ships or air patrols, to avoid being seen. The extra length of the trip meant tankers accompanying the warships had to refuel the ships at sea.

Their target was Pearl Harbor, the base for the American Pacific Fleet, a few miles from Honolulu on the island of Oahu in Hawaii. The Japanese pilots had practiced their attack on a carefully designed model of Pearl Harbor. Japanese spies had told them where every American ship was supposed to be anchored. Each group of pilots had targeted a specific ship. From their spies they knew that most of the antiaircraft guns on the ships and nearby shore installations would not be manned on a Sunday morning, that most of the ships' officers would have spent the night onshore, that the crews would have slept late. Although the threat of war was growing, the United States was still at peace, and security around the base was very careless. Anyone could climb the hills above the harbor and watch with binoculars. All it took was patience and careful observation to learn the American navy's routine.

The fleet stopped about 200 miles from Hawaii and launched its planes on Sunday morning, December 7, 1941.

Just before eight in the morning Hawaii time, the first wave of Japanese planes attacked the anchored American fleet

Although the threat of war was growing, the United States was still at peace, and security around the base at Pearl Harbor was very careless.

Did President Roosevelt Know About Pearl Harbor?

After Pearl Harbor, the United States tried to discover the causes of the disaster. Some people accused President Franklin D. Roosevelt of knowing about the attack before it happened and purposely doing nothing because he wanted the United States to join Britain in the war against Germany. (Similar accusations were made about Roosevelt's handling of relations with Germany. These are discussed on p. 64.)

People who made these accusations pointed to several pieces of evidence. The United States had broken the code used by Japanese diplomats and therefore knew a great deal about Japanese plans. But the military and naval forces did not use this code. American officials believed Japan was preparing for war, but they did not know when or where.

The navy had lined up its battleships in Pearl Harbor like perfect targets, with no protection against torpedoes—in fact, with little protection of any kind. Defensive preparations were completely inadequate; the Japanese destroyed many American planes on the ground. And the American military ignored radar warnings and other signs of the approaching Japanese.

But all of these things are evidence of poor American military preparations, errors in judgment, and carelessness, not of a deliberate plan to allow a Japanese attack. (The British would soon make similar mistakes in Malaya.)

Finally, most historians doubt that Roosevelt would have allowed Japan to destroy the American fleet if his purpose were to get the United States into the war against *Germany.* The American people might have demanded that all resources be used to defeat *Japan,* and might have opposed helping the British fight Germany—the opposite of what Roosevelt wanted. It was only because Germany and Italy declared war on the United States that he never had to face this possibility. Historians generally reject the idea that Roosevelt, or any other American officials, knew about Pearl Harbor beforehand.

and nearby military barracks and airfields. They dropped their torpedoes and dive-bombed their main targets, the eight battleships in the harbor. A second wave of Japanese planes attacked at around 9:00 A.M. and continued the destruction. By the end of the attack, the battleships *Arizona, Oklahoma, California,* and *West Virginia* had sunk, and three others were heavily damaged. Another dozen warships were also hit. Of the nearly 400 American planes based on Oahu, almost 200 were

destroyed and less than 50 survived undamaged. Two thousand four hundred one American sailors and soldiers were killed, and more than 1,100 others were injured.

The USS *Shaw* exploding during the Japanese raid on Pearl Harbor. *(Reproduced by permission of the National Archives and Records Administration)*

The impact of Pearl Harbor

The Japanese attack seemed to have accomplished its purpose. The American Pacific Fleet, the only naval force that

The memorial to the 1,177 sailors who died aboard the USS *Arizona* at Pearl Harbor is visited by 1.5 million people a year. The ship, with the remains of most of the sailors still inside it, lies beneath the memorial. *(Reproduced by permission of the Corbis Corporation [Bellevue])*

could interfere with Japan's plans, was destroyed. In reality, although Pearl Harbor was a military disaster for the United States, it was not the great success for Japan as it first appeared.

First, because the water in Pearl Harbor is so shallow, the Americans could raise all the sunken battleships except the *Arizona* from the bottom and eventually repaired and modernized them. The American battleships were back in service much earlier than anyone expected.

Even more important, the aircraft carriers of the American Pacific Fleet were not in Pearl Harbor at the time of the attack. Two were at sea and one was in California; three other American carriers were in the Atlantic. Within a few months, the aircraft carriers would inflict a major defeat on the Japanese navy.

Finally, the attack on Pearl Harbor had the opposite long-term effect from what Japan wanted. Japanese strategy for winning the war depended on eventually reaching a compromise peace with the United States, and Pearl Harbor made that impossible.

Japan's strategy for the war

Japan's plan was to conquer new territory in Southeast Asia, including Indonesia, the Philippines, and a string of small islands and island groups, some uninhabited, in the Pacific. Japan already controlled some of these islands and could use them as bases from which to attack the others. Japan wanted to conquer most of these small islands not because they contained valuable natural resources or because they were places where Japanese products could be sold. Instead, they were valuable only as military, naval, and air bases.

According to the Japanese strategy, the United States would have to rebuild its navy after Pearl Harbor and then attack these islands one by one. The Japanese believed that the American people would not support a war in which thousands of Americans died to conquer islands that no one had ever heard of. And Americans would oppose sending soldiers to return conquered British and Dutch colonies to the colonial powers when the people of those colonies probably did not want to remain under British or Dutch control.

Instead, the Japanese thought that they could resist the Americans on the Pacific islands long enough to make the United States see that defeating Japan would cost too many lives. Then they would be able to make peace. By then, Japan would have completed its conquest of Southeast Asia and China and could bargain from a position of great strength. The United States would be forced to accept Japan as the dominant power in eastern Asia.

But the Pearl Harbor attack ensured that this would never happen. Americans were furious at the "sneak attack,"

U.S. president Franklin D. Roosevelt signs the declaration of war against Japan, December 8, 1941. *(Reproduced by permission of the National Archives and Records Administration)*

The western Pacific from Hawaii to Japan, 1942.

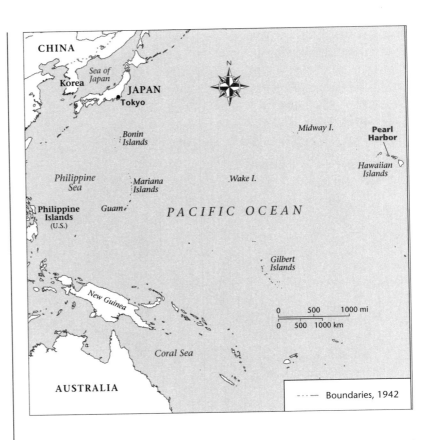

delivered while America was at peace. A whole generation of Americans could say for the rest of their lives where they were when they heard the news of the bombing. They agreed with President Roosevelt when he told Congress that December 7, 1941, was a date that would "live in infamy," meaning that the Japanese attack would always be remembered as a symbol of evil.

It would have been very difficult for the American government—even if it had wanted to—to accept a compromise peace with Japan. Pearl Harbor made most Americans demand the total defeat of Japan. Japanese military and civilian leaders never believed they could defeat the United States in a long, all-out war. They knew American industrial strength was much greater than their own.

Japan sweeps forward

But thoughts of Japan's eventual defeat did not seem very realistic in December 1941. The stunning destruction of the Pacific Fleet was followed by an even more impressive series of Japanese victories. Many of these victories followed a pattern. The Japanese used surprise, great skill, and command of air power to ensure that their forces outnumbered the defenders in a particular area—even if the defenders had more troops altogether. The Japanese troops were well trained and fought with bravery. Their opponents regularly underestimated both the Japanese generals and soldiers. They were constantly amazed by the daring of the Japanese attacks, by their speed, by how carefully planned they were. They were surprised that Japanese military equipment was so advanced, that their planes were better than those of the Western powers, that their pilots flew them so skillfully.

In the western Pacific, Japan moved against two islands belonging to the United States. The day after Pearl Harbor, they attacked the 500 American troops on Guam, who surrendered the following day. The Japanese took the British-held Gilbert Islands on December 9. On tiny Wake Island, a small detachment of U.S. Marines held out until December 23, when their food and water were gone.

Thousands of miles farther west, using troops based in China, the Japanese also attacked the British colony of Hong Kong on December 8. Soon the defenders, including many Canadians, retreated to Hong Kong Island. On December 18, Japanese troops landed on the island, and the 12,000 remaining Allied troops surrendered on Christmas Day.

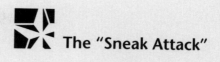

The "Sneak Attack"

One of the things Americans were angriest about was that the attack on Pearl Harbor came before Japan had declared war on the United States. The Japanese government had wanted the attack to come just *after* a declaration of war—so that technically it would not be a "sneak attack." The Japanese had sent a long message in code to its Washington, D.C., embassy, to be delivered to the United States government about half an hour before the attack. The Japanese believed this message amounted to a declaration of war. However, it took longer than expected to decode the message and then translate it into English. By the time they delivered the message, the attack had already begun.

The Philippines

The Japanese attacked the Philippines ten hours after Pearl Harbor (although it was December 8, local time). In that attack, Japanese planes again caught nearly the entire American

Racism

There were several reasons why almost all Americans supported war against Japan. The most important, of course, was the attack on Pearl Harbor. Many Americans had also opposed the Japanese invasion of China and the murder of hundreds of thousands of Chinese civilians. The Japanese government, like those of Germany and Italy, was openly hostile to democracy.

But there was another element in American public opinion. Historians generally agree that anti-Japanese feeling in the United States included strong appeals to racism. American propaganda depicted the Japanese as savages, exaggerating their facial features in cartoons to make them look like monkeys, and described them as sneaky and treacherous people of low intelligence. Even U.S. government officials called them "Japs." American citizens of Japanese ancestry were attacked as they tried to go about their business. Japanese Americans on the West Coast were soon forced from their homes and sent to guarded detention camps (see Chapter 5). Nothing like this happened to Americans whose families had originally come from Germany or Italy. The U.S. government always made it clear that America was fighting Adolf Hitler's Nazis and Benito Mussolini's Fascists, not the German or Italian people. But when it came to Japan, it seemed as if all Japanese were being blamed for attacking the United States, not just their government.

air force on the ground and destroyed it. American warships, lacking planes to protect them from air attack, were ordered to leave the Philippines to help defend the Dutch East Indies.

After several Japanese troop landings on the main Philippine island of Luzon, the American and Filipino troops abandoned the capital city of Manila and retreated to the nearby Bataan Peninsula. The peninsula, less than 30 miles long and perhaps 20 miles wide, was now crowded with American and Filipino soldiers and civilians escaping from Manila. There was a serious shortage of food, and many soldiers became sick. They held off the Japanese for three months. Finally, the Japanese attacked in strength on April 4, 1942, and Bataan surrendered on April 19.

The last major resistance was now on the rocky island of Corregidor. There, 15,000 troops continued to hold out

American troops surrender after the siege of Corregidor. *(Reproduced by permission of the National Archives and Records Administration)*

against constant air attacks and massive artillery shelling from Bataan, 2 miles away. On May 5, Japanese troops with tanks landed on the island against strong American resistance, which caused heavy Japanese casualties. The next day, Corregidor surrendered. In all, the Japanese took 95,000 American and Filipino troops prisoner on Bataan and Corregidor.

Many of these prisoners were forced on a long, brutal march to prison camps. Twenty-five thousand—almost a third of those who started—died from disease, wounds, and mistreatment by their Japanese guards. The "Bataan Death March," as it came to be called, became for many Americans another symbol of Japanese cruelty.

Malaya and Singapore

Japan landed troops in the north of the British colony of Malaya (now part of the country of Malaysia) early on the

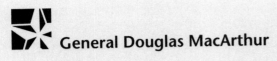

General Douglas MacArthur

The American commander in the Philippines at the time of the Japanese attack was General Douglas MacArthur. MacArthur was probably America's most experienced military officer and had commanded the army in the 1930s. He was a colorful and controversial figure, wearing dark glasses and often smoking a corncob pipe. His opponents thought he was too ambitious and was always seeking publicity.

Later, the Americans "loaned" MacArthur to the government of the Philippines, which was preparing to become independent, to help it build its army. It was only in July 1941, with war threatening, that the Filipino troops and MacArthur again became part of the U.S. Army.

On March 12, 1942, while the Japanese were pressuring Bataan, President Franklin D. Roosevelt ordered MacArthur to leave the Philippines and fly to Australia to take command of the Allied forces in the southwest Pacific. Roosevelt did not want MacArthur captured by the Japanese. As he left, MacArthur promised his troops, "I shall return." In America, where the only war news had been of one defeat after another, MacArthur's words became a symbol of America's determination to win the war, however long it took.

morning of December 8 local time—which was actually an hour before the attack on Pearl Harbor. Although the Japanese were outnumbered, their troops were better trained and had 200 tanks and 560 planes. The British, Australian, Indian, and Malay defenders had no tanks and about 160 mostly outdated planes.

On December 10, the battleship *Prince of Wales,* one of the newest and best ships in the British navy, along with the powerful cruiser *Repulse* tried to intercept Japanese troop transports. Attacked by eighty-five Japanese dive-bombers and torpedo planes, the two ships sank. Despite the ships' powerful antiaircraft guns, the Japanese lost only three planes.

The Allied forces began a general retreat southward down the long Malay peninsula. The Japanese pursued advancing 400 miles through mountains and jungles in only five weeks. By the end of January, they were at the southern end of the peninsula, and the Allied troops were evacuated across the mile-wide strait to the island of Singapore.

Crossing the strait in small boats, the Japanese landed troops on the island on February 8. Although they still outnumbered the Japanese, the Allied troops were demoralized by the long retreat and could not stop them. Fearing for the safety of the 1 million civilians crowded into the city of Singapore, the British commander surrendered on February 15.

Burma and the Dutch East Indies

The Japanese invasion of the British colony of Burma (present-day Myanmar) began in mid-December. Although China sent troops into northern Burma to aid the British, the Japanese continued to advance. By late April, 1942, the Chinese had retreated north back into China, and the British, chased by the Japanese, had crossed into India, the largest and most important British colony.

The Japanese began their invasion of the Dutch East Indies with troop landings on some of the outlying islands, capturing or building airfields to use as bases to continue their advance. As they threatened the most important island, Java, an Allied naval force tried to stop them. Commanded by a Dutch admiral, it included American, British, Dutch, and Australian ships. Beginning on February 27, this fleet engaged a Japanese force of about equal size in the Battle of the Java Sea. The result was another decisive victory for the Japanese navy. The last important Allied naval force for thousands of miles was almost destroyed.

The Japanese could now land forces on Java, and the Dutch and East Indian troops there could not stop them. On

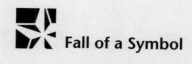

Fall of a Symbol

When Singapore surrendered on February 15, 1942, the Japanese took 130,000 troops prisoner. It was the worst defeat in Britain's long military history. The British had built one of the greatest naval bases in the world in Singapore. But its big guns were designed to defend the island against ships and were not effective against troops on land.

Singapore was the symbol of the British Empire's power in Asia. Many historians believe that the capture of Singapore sent a powerful message to the people of Asia. Even if Britain won the war, the myth that European technology made it impossible for Asians to defeat the European colonial powers was gone forever.

"The Greater East Asia Coprosperity Sphere"

Japan claimed that its purpose in conquering Southeast Asia was to create a "Greater East Asia Coprosperity Sphere." This phrase implied that an association of the people of eastern Asia, under Japanese leadership, would benefit all of them and make them prosperous. Like another Japanese slogan, "Asia for the Asians," it also implied that Japan would lead the Asian people to freedom from the European powers, including Britain, France, and the Netherlands, which had taken away their independence and made them colonies.

Throwing out the European colonial powers was a very popular goal in Asia, especially among the most educated people living in the cities. Independence movements existed throughout the area before the war. The European powers, determined to hold on to their colonies, often made these movements illegal and jailed many of their leaders.

In many places, Japan's defeat of the European powers was welcomed. In some cases, the prewar independence movements cooperated with the Japanese authorities. Japan later officially declared a few of the countries "independent." In reality, however, in all the places the Japanese conquered, they basically replaced the Europeans. The people still were not allowed to make their own decisions. The countries' natural resources were now used for Japan's benefit instead of for the Europeans'. The Japanese authorities—which usually meant army officers—acted like conquerers and treated the local population like inferiors. Japanese rule was often extremely harsh.

March 12, faced with a Japanese threat to bomb the main cities, the Dutch surrendered. In addition to taking military prisoners, the Japanese placed much of the Dutch civilian population, including women and children, in guarded detention camps for the remainder of the war.

Japan now controlled Southeast Asia and all the islands of the western Pacific north of the equator. They had lost only about 15,000 men in all these conquests. The entire Japanese fleet was still afloat; the Allied navies had lost most of their ships. Between Hawaii and Australia, the Japanese controlled the ocean—with one exception. The United States still held the small island of Midway, 1,100 miles west of Hawaii.

The Doolittle raid

Sailing past Midway in April 1942, the American aircraft carrier *Hornet* reached a point about 650 miles from Japan before Japanese boats spotted it and turned it back. But before it did, it launched sixteen B-25 bombers from its decks. The B-25 was a land-based plane. It was really too big and heavy to take off from an aircraft carrier—and impossible to land on one. But it could fly much farther than normal carrier-based bombers.

The commander of the sixteen planes was Colonel James Doolittle, and their mission was to bomb Japan. The B-25s would not have enough fuel to return to the *Hornet*, even if they could find it. The plan was for them to fly to Tokyo and other Japanese cities, drop their bombs, and land in China if they could. On April 18, a dozen of Doolittle's planes bombed three Japanese cities. Four of the planes landed in China; most of the others crashed when they ran out of fuel, but their crews usually parachuted to safety.

The Doolittle raid caused little damage and had no military importance. But Roosevelt wanted some symbolic action to show the American people that the United States was striking back. And it had a great effect on the Japanese military leaders. (Most ordinary people in Japan did not know it had happened.) They were determined to prevent any further strike against the Japanese homeland by destroying the American aircraft carriers that they had failed to find at Pearl Harbor.

The Battle of the Coral Sea

Their first chance came soon. The Japanese planned to land troops in the southern part of the huge island of New Guinea, near Australia, further threatening Australia. The Americans learned of these plans by decoding secret Japanese messages and sent the carriers *Lexington* and *Yorktown* to intercept the invasion, which was protected by three Japanese carriers. On May 7 and 8, planes from the carriers attacked each other's ships. The ships themselves were nearly 200 miles apart. This fight, called the Battle of the Coral Sea, was the first time a naval battle had been fought with the ships apart and not even in one another's sights. When it was over, the *Lexington* had been set on fire and destroyed, one Japanese carrier had been sunk, and another had been heavily damaged. Although neither side won

American sailors abandon the aircraft carrier USS *Lexington*, burning during the Battle of the Coral Sea, May 8, 1942. *(Reproduced by permission of the Corbis Corporation [Bellevue])*

a clear-cut victory, the Japanese threat against northern Australia was greatly reduced.

The Battle of Midway: Luck changes the war

The Japanese navy was now more determined than ever to force an all-out battle with the remaining American carriers. On June 4, 1942, a Japanese invasion fleet approached the island of Midway. It included four large carriers as well as battleships and cruisers. Against them stood the last three American carriers in the Pacific, the *Yorktown, Hornet,* and *Enterprise.* The Americans also had planes based on Midway. For several hours, the planes dueled, trying to attack the enemy's carriers. Eventually, partly by luck, a group of American dive-bombers caught the Japanese carriers while their decks were full of planes being refueled and rearmed, with fuel hoses and bombs lying everywhere. The American bombs started devastating fires. Two Japanese carriers burned and sank. A third was left helpless with no power; an American submarine sank it a short while later. The fourth Japanese carrier tried to escape, but American planes found and destroyed it several hours later.

Military historians consider the Battle of Midway one of the most important naval battles in history and one of the turning points of World War II. Japan had conquered a great empire and could still defend it. But it could no longer expand it, except on land. It could not invade Australia or threaten Hawaii or North America. It would be difficult for Japan to protect the ships that brought oil and other resources from its new empire. After Midway, the United States government could safely use American resources to defeat Germany before turning its attention to Japan.

American strategy

That is exactly what the American government planned to do. Four days after Pearl Harbor, on December 11, 1941, Germany and Italy declared war on the United States. Germany, Italy, and Japan, known as the Axis Powers, signed a treaty in which each promised not to make peace with Britain or the United States without the others.

The United States was now fully in the war, which had truly become a world war. The most important issue facing the American government was whether it should concentrate on the Pacific against Japan or on Europe against Germany. As early as November 1940, American and British military officials had agreed that in a war against the Axis, they would try to defeat "Germany first." In August 1941, Roosevelt had met

After the Battle of Midway, the United States government could safely use American resources to defeat Germany before turning its attention to Japan.

with Winston Churchill, the British prime minister (head of the government), aboard a warship in the North Atlantic. Privately, Roosevelt confirmed the "Germany first" decision.

Soon after Pearl Harbor, Churchill and top British military leaders flew to Washington, D.C., for a series of meetings from December 22 to January 14. The "Germany first" policy became official. The two countries agreed that they would make decisions together on how to use all economic and military resources. They created a joint top command, where the heads of the army, navy, and air force of each country were represented. They set up methods to ensure that they would do all war planning in common.

The two countries made all these decisions while the Japanese army was conquering the Philippines and American public opinion was directed against Japan, only weeks after Pearl Harbor. The "Germany first" strategy made sense for the United States, but it involved some serious military risks in the Pacific, at least until the American victory at Midway. It also involved political risks at home for Roosevelt. Part of the reason he was willing to run those risks was because of the needs of his major allies, Britain and the Soviet Union. The complicated relations between the three countries are described in Chapter 7.

The Home Front | 5

When the war began in Europe in September 1939, the United States had still not fully recovered from the Great Depression that began in the fall of 1929. This was a severe economic crisis marked by falling industrial production and increasing unemployment. (The effects of the depression in Germany are described in Chapter 1.) Although the economy had greatly improved from its low point in 1932, eight million people were still unemployed in 1940, and American industry was still not producing as much as it had been ten years earlier. As many as 40 percent of American families still lived in poverty, on farms as well as in big cities.

In many ways, the 1930s were a decade of turmoil and division in the United States. Workers trying to organize unions clashed with armed company guards and police in many cities. In 1937, there was a wave of "sit-down strikes" involving more than 400,000 workers who took over their workplaces and refused to leave. That spring, Chicago police fired on a crowd of strikers outside a steel mill, killing ten and injuring eighty, in what became known as the "Memorial Day Massacre."

From unemployment to overtime

The coming of World War II changed America in two closely connected ways. It ended the Depression by creating millions of new jobs, and it created a sense of unity in the country. The economic changes came even before the United States entered the war. France and Britain ordered war planes and other weapons from the United States. Soon, American factories and farms were sending their products to Britain in unheard-of quantities. When it looked as if Britain might be unable to pay for further purchases, the United States government, through the Lend-Lease law, in effect loaned Britain money to buy more from American companies. (See Chapter 3.) Although the main reason for this law was to help Britain survive against the Nazis, many people understood that it would also help the American economy.

By the time Japan attacked Pearl Harbor in December 1941 and the United States declared war, America had become "the Arsenal of Democracy," in the phrase made popular by President Franklin D. Roosevelt. Production had grown tremendously, creating more jobs. In addition, the United States had established the first peacetime military draft in its history, so hundreds of thousands of young men who might have been unemployed were now in the army.

After Pearl Harbor, the American economy reached levels that no other country had ever approached. Before the attack, factories had been working at only part of their capacity because they could produce more than they could sell. Now, for many kinds of products, the army or navy ordered more than the factories could make, and new factories had to be built. In 1939, the average American factory was in use forty hours a week. In 1945, it was ninety hours.

Automobile plants assembled tanks, jeeps, and trucks for the military. In fact, as of New Year's Day 1942, a newly created government agency, the Office of Production Management, banned the sale of new private cars or trucks. America turned out 2.4 million military trucks, for the Soviets and British as well as the Americans. The United States produced 86,000 tanks and 6,500 ships to carry goods. It made 15 million rifles and machine guns, 44 *billion* bullets, 400,000 cannons, and 47 million tons of shells for them to fire. Three hundred thousand planes came from the American aircraft industry. Before the war it had employed 46,000 people; by 1945, there were 50 times as many.

The war created whole new industries like synthetic (artificially produced) rubber, because natural rubber came mainly from areas conquered by the Japanese. By 1944, the industry had produced 800,000 tons of it. (A single B-17 bomber used half a ton of rubber.) In the four years of war, the total value of all industrial goods produced in the United States doubled. In 1945, the United States provided one-half of the world's coal and two-thirds of its crude oil.

During the war, average wages in America doubled, from about $25 to $50 a week.

Prosperity

Individual companies produced at levels never seen before. During the war, the United States Steel Corporation made more steel by itself than Germany and Japan combined; the Ford Motor Company alone produced 8,600 bombers, 278,000 jeeps, and 57,000 aircraft engines. Producing greater amounts as fast as possible was more important to the army and navy than efficiency or cost. The government paid these companies on a "cost-plus" basis: it promised to pay them what it cost them to make the product, plus a certain percentage as profit. This meant that companies were guaranteed to make money no matter how much they spent.

And companies' profits increased hugely, although a large share of defense contracts went to only a few dozen large companies. Average wages in America doubled, from about $25 to $50 a week. Overtime work was common and often mandatory in defense industries, so pay there was usually even higher. Total farm income went up two and a half times, even though there were 800,000 fewer agricultural workers. The income of the poorest one-fifth of the population rose 68 percent during the war, more than those who were better off. This meant that there was more economic equality at the end of the war than before.

The federal government spent about $360 billion on the war (about $4.5 *trillion* in 1999 money). Although taxes increased, they only accounted for half this amount, and the government borrowed money to pay for the rest. It did this by selling bonds, which would be repaid with interest later. Banks

Almost no one doubted that the war was necessary, that the United States was fighting for freedom, and that the sacrifices, disruptions, and inconveniences were worth it.

and other financial institutions bought most bonds, but $36 billion in war bonds were sold in small units to the general public. People were urged to show their patriotism by buying war bonds. Bond drives, often featuring Hollywood stars, were common. Children bought "Defense Stamps" in school every week, a nickel or a dime at a time. These campaigns were important economically, but they also made people, including children, feel that they were participating in the war and gave them a greater sense of unity.

Changes and unity

Instead of widespread unemployment, there was soon a labor shortage. New sources of workers had to be found. People from poverty-stricken farm regions, especially in the South, moved to the great industrial cities like Detroit. Large numbers of African Americans were among the many who moved seeking a new life. The aircraft plants of Los Angeles and the naval facilities of San Diego attracted so many new residents that southern California soon became the fastest-growing area of the country. More than 15 million Americans moved during the war, either to find work in war industries or to follow a family member to a new army base within the United States. As millions of men entered the armed services, 6 million women worked outside the home for the first time.

These rapid changes created new problems and new tensions, some of which are described later in this chapter. But they also created a sense of excitement and purpose—and most of all, a sense of unity. Soon after Pearl Harbor, the leaders of America's major unions promised not to strike for the duration of the war. Almost no one doubted that the war was necessary, that the United States was fighting for freedom, and that the sacrifices, disruptions, and inconveniences were worth it. It seemed obvious: the United States had been attacked, Japan and Germany were trying to conquer the world, and only by defending freedom everywhere could the American people preserve their own liberty. Many Americans who lived through World War II always thought of it, in the words of author Studs Terkel, as "the good war."

The Allies needed large numbers of planes, tanks, and other war materials. So instead of widespread unemployment, the United States faced a labor shortage. *(Reproduced by permission of the National Archives and Records Administration.)*

Rationing and government controls

Because America's industrial power was directed toward winning the war, it meant that, despite the incredible amounts produced, there would be domestic shortages of many products that people had taken for granted. There was also a danger that these shortages would cause prices to increase rapidly, canceling out the higher pay that people were

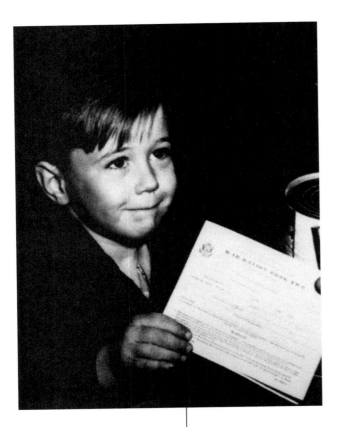

A young boy using a ration slip at a grocery store.
(Reproduced by permission of the National Archives and Records Administration)

earning. The federal government created new agencies with new responsibilities and powers to prevent economic disruptions from interfering with the war effort.

The Office of Price Administration and Civilian Supply (OPA), created in April 1941 a few months after Pearl Harbor, announced rationing of rubber, leading to an 80 percent decline in civilian use. (Rationing meant that people were only allowed to buy a certain amount of a product, even if they could afford more.) Within a month, the OPA was given the power to set prices on all nonagricultural products. In April 1942, it responded to one of the most serious shortages of the war—a lack of adequate housing, especially near new defense plants—with a program of rent stabilization to prevent dramatic rent increases.

In May 1942, sugar was rationed, as was gasoline on the East Coast. Gasoline rationing went nationwide in December. Every car had to display a sticker on its windshield. An "A" sticker meant the car was driven for pleasure only and was entitled to just three gallons of gas a week. The amounts went up from there, with a "B" meaning the car was driven to work and a "C" that it was used on the job. Emergency vehicles got an "E," which entitled them to unlimited purchases of gasoline. Gasoline rationing was very unpopular with Americans, who loved cars, and there was much grumbling and suspicion about anyone who got classified higher than an "A." As was true of other rationed products, people who were willing to pay very high prices could buy extra gasoline illegally. This system of illegal buying and selling is referred to as the black market.

In July 1942, the government introduced a coupon system for rationing. Every family received coupon books, with tiny stamps each worth a certain number of points. They had to turn in the stamps when buying rationed products, each of which cost a set number of points, depending on how scarce it was.

The list of rationed products grew ever longer. Coffee was rationed in November 1942, even though most of it came from Latin America, an area unaffected by the war. But the ships that brought coffee to the United States were more urgently needed elsewhere. Long-distance calls were limited to five minutes. Canned goods were rationed beginning March 1, 1943, and meat, butter, and cheese later that month. Meat was limited to 28 ounces per person a week, and butter to four ounces a week. The "victory gardens" that people were encouraged to grow in every backyard and vacant lot produced 40 percent of all vegetables eaten in the United States in 1942. Victory gardens also created a sense of involvement in the war effort and a feeling of national unity.

Despite all the restrictions, Americans actually ate more and probably better food during the war than at any previous time. This was in contrast with Britain, where people ate less during the war. (See Chapter 8.) It was even more different from the experience of most of Europe, where real hunger and even starvation were common during the war. (See Chapter 6.) The main reason was the increased income of the poorest Americans, a direct result of war jobs.

Rationing Fashion

Shortages and rationing had an impact on many different areas of life. The price of women's silk stockings skyrocketed, and they soon became impossible to find. Most silk had come from Japan, and whatever was still available was used to make parachutes. Nylon stockings had been introduced only a year earlier and had quickly become very popular. But the government took the entire production of nylon for items like tents, airplane tires, and parachutes. Many women began painting black seams on the backs of their legs to make it look as if they were wearing stockings.

Leather was also in short supply, so beginning in February 1943, civilians were limited to three pairs of shoes a year. Wool, cotton, and other materials were needed for uniforms, so the government restricted the fashion industry's designs. A dress could use only one and three-quarter yards of fabric. Men's suits could not be double-breasted

Resentment and conflict

While there was a growing sense of unity, many Americans also resented what they perceived as an inequality in what they had to sacrifice. Anger at the rich and a low opinion

Workers in many industries felt that companies were taking advantage of the war to make money, while ignoring such issues as job safety and fair promotions.

of big business had become common during the Great Depression. Although many people now made more money than they ever had before, they worked long hours, lived in substandard and overcrowded housing, and were severely limited in the consumer products they could buy. In the meantime, they saw companies making record profits and the wealthy apparently able to obtain anything they wanted by paying high prices on the black market.

Workers in many industries felt that companies were taking advantage of the war to make money, while ignoring such issues as job safety and fair promotions. In many cases, workers could not even quit; in April 1943, the government declared 27 million workers "essential," forbidding them to leave their jobs. The push for production led to accidents that caused 17,000 workplace deaths a year and the permanent disabling of 250,000 workers during the war. (Another 4.5 million were less seriously injured.)

Despite the unions' no-strike pledge, there were protest strikes over safety and other issues in many industries. Most were walkouts that occurred against the wishes of union leaders and lasted only a few hours or a couple of days. Some were more substantial, however. In December 1943, the government took over the railroads to prevent a major strike. The president of the coal miners' union, John L. Lewis, called a series of strikes in 1943. (Coal was the most important source of energy and vital to steel production.) Even other union leaders accused Lewis of being a traitor, despite his earlier national popularity.

African Americans and the war

One group that felt both a greater sense of unity and strong resentment was African Americans. Although the war in Europe began to create an economic boom in the United States, African Americans received few of the new jobs. In January 1941, A. Philip Randolph, the organizer and president of the Brotherhood of Sleeping Car Porters, a union of African American railroad workers, organized the March on Washington Movement. The new organization planned to bring thousands of African Americans to a giant demonstration in Washington, D.C. They would demand that the government stop giving defense contracts to companies that discriminated, that the government itself stop discriminating in hiring federal employees, and that the armed forces be integrated.

Afraid of being embarrassed, Roosevelt issued Executive Order 8802 a week before the scheduled march. It stated that the policy of the United States was that there should be no discrimination "in defense industries or government because of race, creed, color, or national origin." Roosevelt also created the federal Fair Employment Practices Commission (FEPC), which was charged with receiving complaints about discrimination and then taking "appropriate steps."

This was the first time since Abraham Lincoln that a president had taken executive action against racial discrimination. Randolph canceled the march but kept the organization together to apply further pressure on the government. Although the FEPC's enforcement powers turned out to be quite limited, the defense industries hired significant numbers of African Americans. In general, however, they were limited to the dirtiest, lowest-paying jobs. The armed forces remained completely segregated.

Before Pearl Harbor, some sections of the African American community were less pro-British than many American whites. This was mainly because the United States's ally was a great colonial power, with hundreds of millions of non-white people in Asia and Africa living in countries that Britain controlled for its own benefit. Some African Americans considered the struggle for the independence of these countries, such as India, similar to their own struggle for equal rights in America. (Britain's colonial history also made other groups, such as Irish Americans, less pro-British before Pearl Harbor.)

But once the United States entered the war, the African American community strongly supported the war effort. Many African Americans thought that the fight against Nazi racism in Europe should be joined to the fight against racism and discrimination in America. This was symbolized by the "Double-V" campaign, begun by the *Pittsburgh Courier*, an African American newspaper, in 1942. The "V for Victory" sign was doubled to signify that African Americans were fighting for democracy both overseas and at home.

Many African Americans thought that the fight against Nazi racism in Europe should be joined to the fight against racism and discrimination in America.

MILITARY POLICE
COLORED

Black soldiers serving during World War II were completely segregated from white troops and most received non-combat assignments. *(Reproduced by permission of the National Archives and Records Administration.)*

African Americans and the armed services

Although the law that set up the military draft, the Selective Service Act, banned discrimination, both the Navy Department and the army's War Department ignored this. (After World War II, the Departments of War and the navy merged to form the Department of Defense.) The War Department claimed that allowing African Americans to serve equally would lower the morale (spirit or willingness to fight) of white soldiers. Both Secretary of War Henry Stimson and Army Chief of Staff General George C. Marshall believed that white soldiers might refuse to fight alongside blacks. Many top officials also believed, without any supporting evidence, that African Americans were not brave and disciplined enough to serve in combat units, even if they were segregated from whites.

The predraft army was overwhelmingly white. There were about 5,000 black soldiers and a few dozen black officers in an army of about 100,000 men. The Marine Corps and the air force did not accept any African Americans at all. The peacetime army did not encourage African Americans to join until after Pearl Harbor, when the need for men grew.

Even then, African Americans were almost never placed in combat units, infantry, armored, or artillery. Instead, they were concentrated in service units, troops who unloaded supplies, maintained vehicles, built barracks on army bases, and did all the other work an army needs. By the end of 1944, there were 700,000 African Americans in the army (about 9 percent of the total) and about 5,000 African American officers. Although a majority were serving overseas, they were still almost all in service units.

African American combat units

However, there were three segregated black combat divisions (a large army unit, usually about 15,000 men), the Ninety-Second and Ninety-Third Infantry Divisions and the Second Cavalry Division. (Cavalry divisions were now "mounted" on jeeps and other vehicles, not on horses.) Although all the soldiers, corporals, and sergeants were African American, all the top officers were white. The Second Cavalry was disbanded, and the Ninety-Third Division served in the Pacific but saw little combat. The Ninety-Second Division fought in Italy and saw much more action, with 600 men killed and another 2,000 wounded. However, its commander was a white general who openly distrusted the ability of African American troops. In return, the soldiers had no confidence in their officers. The unit developed a poor reputation as a result.

Very different was the reputation of the 761st Tank Battalion, a segregated armored unit that fought mainly in France and Germany, as part of General George Patton's Third Army. From the time it entered combat in November 1944 until Germany's surrender the following May, the unit fought for 183 consecutive days. It played an important role in defeating the last German counteroffensive, the Battle of the Bulge. (See Chapter 12.) Despite this record, it did not receive a Presidential Unit Citation until 1978.

The peacetime army did not encourage African Americans to join until after Pearl Harbor, when the need for men grew. Even then, African Americans were concentrated in service units.

African American soldiers stand at attention while an officer reviews the troops. The U.S. armed forces remained segregated throughout the war.
(Reproduced by permission of the National Archives and Records Administration.)

The navy and the air force

Discrimination was even worse in the navy. Traditionally, African Americans had only been allowed to work in ships' kitchens and to serve food to the officers in their dining areas. During World War II, 95 percent of African American sailors onboard ships were still limited to these jobs. Onshore, large numbers of African American sailors were used as laborers, to load ships and transport material. The WAVES, the women's naval corps, did not accept any African American women until 1944. In that year, the navy finally allowed African American seamen to serve on 25 "white" ships. At that time, there were 165,000 African Americans in the navy and about 17,000 in the Marine Corps.

The air force created some all-black squadrons under orders, but most of them were used to maintain airfields. The first African American airmen to see action were members of the Ninety-Ninth Fighter Squadron, which flew in Italy beginning in April 1943. Commanded by Benjamin O. Davis, who later became the air force's first African American general, this unit became famous as the Tuskegee Airmen (after the Alabama town where they were trained). But it was an exception, which white air force officers tried to end. Only three other African American squadrons were allowed in combat.

Heroes and riots

The military's discriminatory policies made it more difficult to convince African Americans that the war was being fought for freedom. In one well-known incident, African American troops watched in amazement as a restaurant in a small Kansas town served lunch to German prisoners of war but refused to serve black American soldiers. African American soldiers returning from overseas on leave were sent to different—and inferior—hotels. With the cooperation of the American Red Cross, the army even segregated blood supplies of whites and African Americans.

There were often tensions between African American and white units, especially on bases in the segregated South. There were even several small-scale riots on bases. The army tried to keep its own facilities, such as officers clubs, racially segregated even on bases in northern states, where segregation was against the law. In fact, white soldiers tried to introduce segregated facilities near American bases in England, causing fights to break out.

At the same time, the government was urging African Americans to participate in the war effort. Posters even featured heavyweight boxing champion Joe "the Brown Bomber" Louis, now a private in the army, who was tremendously popular among African Americans.

Discrimination was even worse in the Navy.

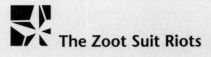

The Zoot Suit Riots

For several days in June 1943, hundreds of cars and taxis filled mostly with white sailors drove through the Mexican American neighborhoods of Los Angeles, attacking young men dressed in "zoot suits." Zoot suits had extra-long jackets with shoulder pads. The pants were baggy at the knee and tapered down to the ankle. Large hats and pocket watches on long chains were also part of the look.

The zoot suit was as different as could be from a trim military uniform. According to some experts, this contrast was the reason for its popularity among young Mexican Americans in Los Angeles. Some of the zoot-suiters were in social clubs, and some were in street gangs. Rumors that zoot-suiters had attacked servicemen were the trigger for the attacks. The sailors beat up "zooters" and other Mexican Americans, cut their hair, and ripped off their clothes. The Los Angeles police stood by watching the beatings and then often arrested the zoot-suiters. The newspapers blamed the zooters for the riots, and the city council made it a criminal offense to wear a zoot suit in public.

Another African American used to encourage recruitment was Dorie Miller, a sailor who had been a mess steward (kitchen worker) aboard the battleship USS *Arizona,* sunk at Pearl Harbor. Miller shot down two attacking Japanese planes with a machine gun, and received the Navy Cross, the navy's second-highest medal after the Congressional Medal of Honor. (Miller was killed two years later when the Japanese sank the escort carrier USS *Liscome Bay.*)

During the war, 700,000 African Americans, many from the South, moved to industrial cities. Sixty thousand moved to Detroit alone, and 1.2 million nationwide now worked in industrial jobs. Some white workers, many of them also recent arrivals from the South, resented working with African Americans. Sometimes white workers walked off the job to protest promotion of African Americans. Tensions over crowded housing in the industrial cities added to the strain.

Detroit Riot In June 1943, a series of fights between blacks and whites at a city park in Detroit grew into a major riot when nearby white sailors joined in. That night, groups of African Americans attacked stores and streetcars. Two whites, including a milkman and a doctor making a house call, were beaten to death. The next day, mobs of whites began attacking any African American they could find. Troops were called in to end the chaos, but a total of 34 people, 25 of them African Americans, were killed and 700 injured.

Harlem Riot A smaller riot occurred in the Harlem neighborhood of New York City in August 1943, when a false rumor spread that a white police officer had shot and killed an African American soldier. Five people were killed and nearly four hundred injured.

Women in industry

Some of the most dramatic changes in wartime concerned the role of women in society. As production expanded and men were drafted into the army, more women than ever before entered the workforce.

Some of these women were secretaries and clerical workers, as they had always been. But for the first time, large numbers were given jobs welding and operating lathes and other industrial machinery. The symbol of the woman war worker in industry was Rosie the Riveter, who used a rivet gun to join together the metal plates of airplane bodies or ships' sides.

Poster recruiting women to work. *(Reproduced by permission of the Corbis Corporation [Bellevue])*

Although the work was often dirty and dangerous, many women found—to their surprise—that it did not require an exceptionally large or strong person. For example, relatively small women could use a welding torch. Of course, their arms would get tired—but that was true of men as well. Women, who had always been told that they lacked natural mechanical aptitude, were quickly trained to be drafters and designers and to operate complicated machinery. Despite the fact that they often did the same jobs as men, they were rarely paid the same. In general, women only earned about two-thirds as much as men.

United States

The number of women working outside the home in the United States rose by more than 6 million, a 50 percent increase. By 1944, about 60 percent of American women— around 19 million—worked outside the home, including 25 percent of married women. By the end of the war, women con-

stituted more than one-third of the American civilian workforce. According to a government survey, 80 percent of those women, including almost 70 percent of those who were married, wanted to continue working after the war.

Almost 6 million of the women were working in factory jobs. The number of women working in aircraft factories rose from 143 in 1941 to around 65,000 at the end of 1942.

Children First?

Many people feared that women would become toughened by factory work and that their femininity and morality would suffer. The U.S. government reminded women that taking care of children, even in wartime, was still their most important job. But although 2.75 million American women workers had children under the age of fourteen, there was a severe shortage of day-care facilities. Many children had to be cared for by grandparents or neighbors, or left alone.

The war affected American children in other ways. Because many of the 16 million American men in the military had children, almost 20 percent of families were separated during the war. The labor shortage also led to a loosening of restrictions on child labor, and the higher pay encouraged them to get jobs.

Many families could not survive on the low pay that soldiers received, and this further encouraged both women and children to enter the workforce. By 1944, 20 percent of boys aged fourteen and fifteen had jobs, as did 40 percent of those sixteen and seventeen. One-third of sixteen- to eighteen-year-old girls worked. More than one-third of both boys and girls aged sixteen to eighteen had dropped out of school to work full-time. The lowering of the graduation rate reversed a longtime trend in the United States. Some people were concerned about changes in teenagers' behavior. They worried about increasing loss of parental control, use of "adult language," and increased sexual activity. Others have said that what was seen as a decline in morality was really just teenagers' greater independence.

Eventually, more than half the workers in the giant Boeing aircraft plant near Seattle were women.

The government was anxious to encourage women to enter the workplace. Rosie the Riveter was featured on posters and in a song. Everywhere, women were told that it was patriotic to work in a factory and that calling in sick was a betrayal of the soldiers fighting in the Pacific. Women in shipyards were "soldiers without guns," the heroines of the "Ships for Victory" program. The film star Veronica Lake cut off her much-imitated long, peekaboo-style hair because it was considered a safety hazard for women working with machines. Instead of skirts, women wore trousers or—for the first time—jeans.

On the large factorylike farms that dominated Soviet agriculture, women made up 80 percent of the workers during World War II.

Soviet Union

In the Soviet Union, the most important change in women's roles was the huge increase in the number of women working in war industries and other heavy industry. In the Soviet Union, one million women joined the paid workforce in the first six months after the German invasion. By the end of the war, women made up 55 percent of the Soviet workforce, compared with 30 percent before the war. On the large factorylike farms that dominated Soviet agriculture, they made up 80 percent of the workers.

Great Britain

In Great Britain, the number of women working outside the home grew from around 5 million in 1939 to 7.75 million in 1943. This was the largest percentage increase of any country in the war. Even this number disguises how big the change really was because many women who already had jobs in traditional women's industries, such as cloth and clothing manufacturing or as domestic servants, switched to jobs in heavy industry. Two million women worked in war industries, including shipbuilding, chemicals, and vehicle and aircraft production, four times as many as at the beginning of the war.

Although patriotic feelings and good pay certainly encouraged many women to do this, the British government also used the law to increase their numbers. Starting in March 1941, British women could legally be "directed" into war work. This law eventually covered most women under the age of 50, including married women, but not those with young children. (Day-care provisions were never adequate for the children whose mothers chose to work in industry.)

Germany

Although large numbers of German women worked outside the home before the war, making up 37 percent of the workforce, Hitler did not want to encourage any further increase. Many people think this was mainly because the Nazis were generally very conservative about what roles women should play in society. Many Nazis thought they should be limited to three areas: *"Kinder, Küche, Kirche"* ("children, kitchen, church"). Another major factor in not urging German women to take jobs was Hitler's concern about interfering with German civilian life too much and losing political support. The Nazis were considerably more afraid than the British and American governments of changing the German economy to one of total war—in which industry, most resources, and the labor force is devoted to teh war effort—and disrupting civilian life.

Slave labor Instead, Germany tried to solve its wartime labor shortage by using millions of foreign workers, most of them forced or slave workers. The first large group of these workers were Poles, both prisoners of war and civilians who were drafted. At first, most replaced German farmworkers, who could then work in factories or enter the army. By the end of 1941, the Poles made up about one-half of the almost 4 million foreign workers in Germany, many of whom were now working in factories. These included some who came voluntarily: Italians, Frenchmen, Belgians, and other western Europeans who could not find work in their home countries, which were conquered or dominated by Germany. But they were not really free. These foreign workers could not change jobs or go home unless they had permission. Eventually, the differences between them and the forced laborers almost disappeared.

There were more than 6 million foreign workers by the spring of 1943. Almost none of the 2 million new workers were volunteers. Although the Germans introduced mandatory labor service in France and other western European countries, the largest number were from the conquered areas of the Soviet Union, with a total of about 1.5 million. The number of foreign workers in Germany reached an incredible 7 million—about one-fifth of the total German labor force—in the middle of 1944. (Seven million more people worked for Germany in their home countries, either in German-controlled factories or building military fortifications.)

Almost every sizable factory in Germany included forced labor in its workforce. Camps or barracks to house the workers were in almost every German city. (Because their housing was often located near factories, the forced laborers were frequently the victims of Allied bombings.) The conditions workers faced were horrible. They worked long hours at difficult jobs without enough food. The Germans could severely punish them for disobeying orders, and thousands were shot. The large number of women, most of them from the Soviet Union, were forcibly sterilized.

Almost every sizable factory in Germany included forced labor in its workforce.

Children also contributed to the homefront war effort.

Japan

Of all the major countries involved in World War II, Japan alone did not allow women to join any branch of its armed services. The number of Japanese women working in factories increased only slightly during the war. This was partly because Japan's leaders did not want to change the traditional roles of men and women. But it was also because many Japanese women already worked on family farms. Their labor became even more important while the men were away in the war.

The Japanese also made extensive use of forced labor. They forced Allied prisoners of war to perform backbreaking work in unbearable heat with inadequate food or medical attention. Projects such as building a railroad from Thailand to Burma have become well-known in Western countries because of books and movies like *The Bridge on the River Kwai*. Out of the 61,000 Allied prisoners who worked building this road, almost one-fifth died. Despite this number, Allied prisoners were not the major source of Japanese forced labor. Two hundred seventy thousand Asians, mostly Thais and Burmese, were forced to work on the railroad, and 90,000 of them—one out of three—died. The Japanese forced hundreds of thousands of Koreans to work in Japan and forced Korean women to be prostitutes for the Japanese army.

Children's roles

Children also contributed to the homefront war effort. In Britain, for example, they helped their parents plant victory gardens in every backyard and on the edge of every village. The potatoes and vegetables they grew helped reduce Britain's need to import food past the German submarines that patrolled the Atlantic.

Children also took part in scrap drives—campaigns to collect old metal articles. They went door to door collecting pots and pans, old washbasins, and every other kind of metal object. Iron and steel items were melted down and used to make steel for ships and weapons; copper was used for electric wire. (Children in the United States also participated in scrap drives.)

Japanese Americans

Japanese Americans were treated very poorly during World War II. At the beginning of the war, 127,000 Americans of Japanese background (less than one-tenth of 1 percent of the population) lived in the United States. Eighty thousand of them, known as Nisei, had been born in the country and so were American citizens. The rest, called Issei, were born in Japan. They were the parents of the Nisei and had lived in America for many years, since before a 1924 law had stopped almost all Japanese immigration into the United States. The same law also prevented the Issei from becoming American citizens.

All but 15,000 Japanese Americans lived on the West Coast, especially in California. They had long been the victims of discrimination, including laws that made it illegal for them to marry whites and barred them from some public places like swimming pools. Some state laws kept Japanese Americans from owning land and prevented Nisei from voting.

Partly because of this discrimination, the Issei were less integrated into mainstream American society than some other immigrant groups, especially those from Europe. They still spoke mainly Japanese, ate Japanese food, and observed Japanese holidays. This was also true, although to a lesser extent, of the Nisei.

Most Japanese Americans worked in a few industries. They were small farmers, usually renting their land, and raising such crops as lettuce and green beans that were sold locally. These farmers were an important part of the California economy. Other Japanese Americans were fishermen or owned small stores. Very few were in other businesses or professions like law or medicine, or worked in factories. In many ways, therefore, Japanese Americans were isolated from other Americans. The discrimination against them helped ensure that they would have few allies, that they were seen as different and outsiders.

Racism and Pearl Harbor

Japanese American isolation and the anti-Asian racism that was common in the United States contributed to what happened to them during the war. The spark was the Japanese attack on Pearl Harbor. American hatred against Japan and its

Partly because of this discrimination, the Issei were less integrated into mainstream American society than some other immigrant groups, especially those from Europe.

This window display has a caricature of a Japanese soldier that was common during the war. Japanese Americans faced the same racism and stereotyping as the Japanese. *(Reproduced by permission of the Corbis Corporation [Bellevue])*

"sneak attack" was commonly combined with racist ideas that portrayed the Japanese as shifty and treacherous people of low intelligence. They were depicted as cruel savages, their facial features exaggerated in cartoons to make them look like monkeys.

It did not take long to extend these racist ideas to Japanese Americans. Newspapers and local politicians whipped up hysteria against them. The governor of Idaho said that "Japs live like rats, breed like rats, and act like rats." The main argument was that their loyalty to the United States could not be trusted, that some of them would help Japan by spying on American defenses or sabotaging (intentionally destroying) military facilities.

Local politicians demanded the removal of all 112,000 Japanese Americans from the West Coast, even though there was not a single known case of spying or sabotage. Some military leaders realized this was nonsense. If there had really been a danger of Japanese American disloyalty, the place where it would have caused a serious problem was Hawaii, where one-third of the population was of Japanese descent. The threat of further Japanese attacks in Hawaii was far more realistic than an invasion of California. In fact, Hawaii was placed under martial law (military law, with many normal legal rights suspended). But there were no extra restrictions on people of Japanese ancestry in Hawaii.

Other military authorities, however, agreed with the newspapers that there was no difference between the Japanese in Japan and American citizens of Japanese background. "A Jap's a Jap," said General John L. DeWitt, military commander for the West Coast.

Relocation

On February 19, 1942, President Franklin D. Roosevelt issued Executive Order 9066, which authorized the War Department to classify any-place in the country as a military area, and then to bar any persons they chose from those areas. This authority was used only for the states of California, Oregon, and Washington, and the only people excluded were Japanese Americans—*all* Japanese Americans.

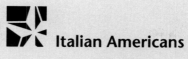

Italian Americans

The U.S. government's treatment of Italian Americans was in sharp contrast to its treatment of Japanese Americans. There were 600,000 Italian American immigrants, mostly on the East Coast, who were not citizens. They were classified as enemy aliens after Italy declared war on the United States, three days after Pearl Harbor. Those who wanted to become American citizens could not, and they were subject to some restrictions on their right to travel. Only a tiny handful who were actually suspected of being spies were arrested. The millions of Italian Americans who were citizens were not restricted in any way.

Even the relatively minor restrictions on the noncitizens did not last long. Although America remained at war with Italy, President Franklin D. Roosevelt removed Italian Americans from the category of enemy aliens ten months after Pearl Harbor, on Columbus Day 1942.

On March 31, Japanese Americans in the three states had to register at control stations. They were then told when to report for relocation to an internment camp. It is fairly common to intern citizens of an enemy country in wartime, which means to place them in some sort of guarded facility. This is especially true for people who actually live in the enemy country and are planning to return to their home. The Issei, however, were immigrants to the United States who planned to remain for the rest of their lives. Even more important, the

A Japanese American family reports for relocation.
(Reproduced by permission of the Library of Congress)

Nisei were American citizens, with the same legal and constitutional rights as all other Americans.

The Japanese Americans were told they would be moved anywhere from four days to two weeks later. They could bring only what they could carry. In that short time, they had to sell the rest of their property for whatever they could get. Many people took advantage of their Japanese American neighbors to buy their homes, stores, or cars at very low prices.

The camps

Armed soldiers moved the Japanese American families from their homes to receiving stations, such as fairgrounds or racetracks where families might be housed in horse stalls. From there they were sent to a relocation camp. There were eventually ten of these camps, all but one in the far west (the exception was in Arkansas). All were located in remote areas unsuitable for farming, surrounded by fences, and guarded by the army. The best known was Manzanar in the southern California desert. A total of 120,000 people lived in the ten camps during the course of the war.

People lived in long wooden barracks divided into one-room apartments, in which an entire family lived. There was almost no furniture and only a bare bulb for light. Toilets, bathing facilities, and dining areas were shared by many families. Although half the Nisei were under eighteen years old when they were relocated, the government had not planned for adequate schools. Recreation facilities hardly existed. There was no work and few ways to pass the time. The relocation camps were like medium-security prisons—except that the prisoners' only crime was their Japanese ancestry.

Release from the camps was possible if someone could show that he or she was loyal to the United States and had a job waiting in a community that was willing to accept the applicant. This turned out to be almost impossible, and most of the Japanese Americans who were temporarily released from the camps in 1943, between 15,000 and 20,000 people, were students.

The Japanese Americans' anger at their treatment was mixed with a desire to prove themselves. When Nisei were made eligible to join the armed services in 1943, about three-quarters of the young men did join and fought bravely, even while their parents were still being held in camps. The 442nd Infantry Regiment, a segregated unit made up entirely of Nisei that fought in Italy, won more medals than any other unit in the U.S. Army. About one-quarter, however, refused to swear allegiance to the United States. Some even renounced (gave up) their American citizenship.

During the war, the United States Supreme Court rejected legal challenges to the exclusion and internment policy. Almost all legal experts now believe that these cases were among the lowest moments in the court's history. The exclusion order was repealed in January 1945. In 1959, American citizenship was restored to those Nisei who had renounced it. In 1989, a federal law provided $20,000 to each surviving victim. And in 1993, a court ruled that interning the Japanese Americans had violated their constitutional rights.

The relocation camps were like medium-security prisons—except that the prisoners' only crime was their Japanese ancestry.

Europe Under Occupation

6

Because World War II was a total war, its effects on ordinary people, not just the soldiers and sailors, were deeper and more widespread than in previous wars. This was especially true when a foreign army defeated and then occupied a country. A military occupation, when one country stations troops on another's territory to control it, is often a time of hardship. But occupation by Nazi Germany in World War II was much harder and more murderous than anything that had come before. While Germany occupied or controlled much of Europe from 1940 to the middle of 1944, it carried out policies, especially in eastern Europe, that involved the intentional killing of millions of people.

Even in western and northern Europe, where occupied countries were treated relatively mildly at the beginning, the Germans used the economic resources of the conquered country for the benefit of Germany. The impact on the local population was lower wages, less food, poorer health, and sometimes forced labor in Germany. In other places, especially in eastern and southeastern Europe, German economic policy amounted to stealing everything they could and leaving as little as possible for the locals, who were essentially treated as slaves.

Economic gains were not the only reason Germany occupied countries. Indeed, German treatment of the occupied Soviet Union, which amounted to looting and smashing everything of value, produced fewer economic benefits for Germany than it received from the smaller and less populous France. In fact, Germany got more farm and other products from the Soviet Union before it invaded, by buying them.

Germany's long-term goal in eastern Europe was the permanent destruction of the nations it conquered. This did not mean simply dominating their governments, as in France. It meant wiping out the very idea of a country separate from German control. Sometimes German leaders actually described their goal as the creation of a slave empire.

This goal was closely tied to Nazi racial theories. The Nazis believed that Germans were a master "race," superior to all others, and had a right to attack, conquer, and enslave weaker ones. Adolf Hitler, the absolute ruler of Nazi Germany, believed that Germany needed *Lebensraum,* or "room to live." This word implied that without more land, Germany could not survive. Hitler believed that this new land should come from eastern Europe. Germany would take over the area and populate it with Germans. The Poles, Russians, Ukrainians, White Russians, and others who already lived there would serve the German overlords as sources of cheap labor. Any who resisted this fate would be killed. Millions of others would die from lack of adequate food, shelter, and medicine. And, according to Nazi racial theories, the millions of Jews who lived in these areas were not even people but "subhumans" who would all be killed. (The Nazi attempt to destroy the Jews, known as the Holocaust, was not limited to eastern Europe. It is described in Chapter 7.)

The way the Germans treated captured Soviet soldiers is an example of how Nazi ideas about race led to inhumanly cruel actions that made no economic sense. More than 5.5 million Soviet troops were captured beginning in June 1941, more than 3 million of them in the first few months of the German invasion. An estimated 1 million of these soldiers died before they reached any kind of prison camp, often shot by the German troops to whom they surrendered. Another 2 million died in the German camps, where they were crowded together with no shelter—and often no food whatsoever. In some camps, there were reports of cannibalism, as the starving soldiers ate the flesh of those who had already died. Another quarter-million died while the Germans transported them from one place to another, some of them forced to march until they died.

Poland

The Nazis began putting some of their plans into action as soon as they conquered Poland in September 1939. Desirable parts of western Poland were annexed to (made part of) Germany. The Nazis intended to force all Poles out of these areas and replace them with *Volksdeutsche,* people with German ancestors who lived outside Germany, often for many generations. The Nazi plan meant moving millions of people from their homes, most of them against their will. The Nazis acted very quickly, but with little preparation. People had almost no time to get ready. They could take little food with them and had to leave almost all their household belongings. In reality, they were being robbed of their property, as well as being forced from their homes. Among the 2 million Poles forced to leave were about 600,000 Jews, who were specially targeted.

The Germans forced the Poles into the part of German-occupied Poland that had not been annexed, which the Germans called the General Government. The Nazis did not want to make the General Government part of Germany. Instead, they wanted to destroy it as a nation and run it for the benefit of Germany. Hitler told Hans Frank, the man he picked to run the General Government, that his job was to turn Poland's "economic, cultural, and political structure into a heap of rubble."

On October 3, 1939, only days after Poland's defeat, Frank told officers of the German army how he planned to achieve these ends. He would "remove all supplies, raw materials, machines, factories, installations, etc. which are important for the German war economy." He would reduce the Polish economy to the absolute minimum necessary for the "bare existence of the population," he said. "The Poles shall be the slaves of the Greater German World Empire." The German policy was to send everything of value back to Germany. Factories that were not stripped of their machines were to be run by Germans.

The Nazis planned to destroy the educational system in Poland and the occupied areas of the Soviet Union.

Destroying the nation

The economic plundering was only part of the plan to destroy Poland. The Nazis wanted to eliminate anyone who might be a leader of any type, which included all educated Poles. The first wave of terror began immediately and resulted in the murder of 60,000 Poles and the imprisonment of thousands more.

The *Einsatzgruppen* ("special-action groups" or "special-duty groups") committed most of the killings. These specially trained strike forces were like a combination of army troops and secret police officers. The *Einsatzgruppen* followed the regular German army closely, arriving in towns immediately after the army entered them. They killed Polish political leaders, even those who shared some of the Nazis' ideas. They killed members of the Polish nobility. They killed doctors, lawyers, professors, high-school teachers, and people with technical training. They killed many priests, who were often community leaders in heavily Catholic Poland. In the Archdiocese (church district) of Poznan, in the annexed part of Poland, there were 681 priests and 147 monks when the Germans arrived. By October 1941, 74 had been shot, 120 had been expelled to the General Government, and 451 were in jail or concentration camps, the brutal prison camps run by the SS (stands for *schutzstaffel,* the German name for the black-uniformed military branch of the Nazi Party).

To make sure that these educated people were never replaced, the Nazis planned to destroy the educational system in Poland and the occupied areas of the Soviet Union. A secret report to Hitler from Heinrich Himmler, the head of the SS, said that schools for the non-German population of these areas should be limited to four-grade elementary schools. The children were to learn only "simple arithmetic up to 500 at the most," the ability to write their names, and that God wanted them to obey the Germans and to be "honest, industrious, and good." No conquering country in modern history had ever made plans like this. Throughout these areas, the Germans simply closed down most schools. In the city of Vilna in 1943, there was one primary school for a Polish population of 104,000. In response, the Poles created secret schools, including a university with 2,500 students that even issued degrees to its graduates.

The secret university was part of a widespread network of secret organizations that engaged in many different activities to resist the Germans. In Poland, as in the rest of Europe, these organizations became known as the underground or the resistance. One was the Home Army (*Armia Krajowa,* known as the AK), which eventually had 300,000 members and fought an armed rebellion in Warsaw in August 1944. (The Warsaw uprising is described in Chapter 12.) The Polish underground published more than 1,000 newspapers and magazines. Three hundred of these came out regularly throughout the occupation. The underground also published books, including scholarly works that were not related to the war. Despite Hitler's orders to turn Poland "into a heap of rubble," the Poles were determined to preserve their culture and traditions.

Germany actually made a profit from occupying countries.

Western Europe: Legalized theft

Instead of the smash-and-grab methods they used in eastern Europe, the Germans developed more complicated ways of stealing in western Europe. One was simply to force the occupied country to pay the cost of the occupation. These costs were figured according to how wealthy the country was, not what it really cost to keep the German army there. So Germany actually made a profit from occupying countries. France, the richest and largest country Germany conquered, paid millions of dollars a day, more than half of all payments the Germans received.

Another method was to set the value of German money, the mark, at a high rate compared with the local currency. This meant that German companies and the German government could buy local products with fewer marks—in other words, they artificially lowered the price for purchases with German money. Throughout western Europe, German companies were soon buying local businesses. More and more of an occupied country's economy fell into German hands. Germany even used similar methods with its allies, such as Hungary and Romania. It was almost impossible to refuse these deals because, behind Germany's economic demands, there was always the threat of military force.

Food shortages

One of Germany's major goals was to ensure that it could send home a steady supply of farm products, which also caused food shortages in the occupied countries. The shortages were made worse by Allied bombing of railroad and road systems, which made it more difficult to get food from farms to people in the cities. Everywhere, food and other products were rationed, which means the amounts that people could buy were limited. The idea behind the rationing was that everyone could get their share. In fact, however, the shortages led to high prices and to illegal buying and selling on the black market. People with enough money could buy more than their share illegally. Others might not get enough to eat.

The official rations were different in various countries and at different times. Germany had the most rations. Almost everywhere else, people ate much less than before the war, generally about one-half to two-thirds as much. In France, the official ration provided around 1,200 calories a day, but even this much was not always available except on the black market. For example, in Paris the official price of butter in 1941 was 40 francs a kilogram (2.2 pounds). By 1943, this had gone up to 61 francs. But the real price that people actually had to pay to get butter in 1943 was 800 francs. In the same way, products like wine and tobacco had an official price, but the real price was ten or twelve times as high. A meal in a factory's lunchroom, where prices were supposed to be kept low, cost the company's workers a full day's pay. Throughout the war, some foods, like meat, were especially scarce. Often meat could not be bought in Paris for an entire month.

Sometimes the ration was much lower. In the Greek capital of Athens in the winter of 1941–42, the average adult was getting 600 to 800 calories a day, which led to widespread malnutrition, illness, and death. (One peanut butter sandwich on white bread contains more than 350 calories.) In those parts of the Netherlands that were still occupied by Germany, the winter of 1944–45 was known as the "hunger winter." People consumed about 500 calories a day, and many starved.

A harder life

It was not just food that was expensive. In France in 1943, a pair of shoes cost what the average person earned in six weeks. (This would be like a pair of shoes in the United States in 1999 costing about $4,000.) A man's suit in Paris cost about four months' pay. Coal was so expensive that most people could not afford enough to cook their meals.

Winters bring disease

Because both clothing and fuel for heating were expensive and hard to find, each winter brought terrible suffering in northern areas. It was made worse by the fact that people were often malnourished. Not surprisingly, there was a general decline in health. There were outbreaks and sometimes epidemics of tuberculosis, diptheria, typhus, typhoid, and cholera. At the end of the war, there were 1.5 million cases of tuberculosis in Poland—an incredible 6 percent of the surviving population. Shortages of medicine made it difficult to control these diseases. In places such as France where reliable statistics exist, it is known that there was a serious increase in death rates, especially of infants.

Death could come more suddenly as well. Although people in occupied Europe welcomed the sight of British and American planes on their way to bomb Germany, many of the raids were aimed at factories in occupied countries. The first successful large-scale British bombing raid in Europe was on the Renault factory complex in a Paris suburb in March 1942. It resulted in large numbers of civilian deaths.

Crime increases

Life was harder in other ways, too. As hunger grew in most countries, there was a large increase in crime, especially theft and prostitution, even though the police had more power to stop and arrest people. There were virtually no private cars, and train travel was restricted. There was usually a curfew, and no one was allowed out at night. People were not allowed to visit or move to another city without permission. Everyone had to have an identity card, which the police could check at any time. Attendance at sports events and movies increased, however, as people looked for escapist entertainment to help them forget about the war. Although most films made during the war were either pure escapism or pro-German propaganda, a few, especially in France, were very good, even great, films that are still valued today.

As hunger grew in most countries, there was a large increase in crime.

Censorship

People in occupied countries had to be careful about expressing their opinions. Criticizing the Germans or the government that was cooperating with them could mean jail or even deportation to a concentration camp. The police often read and censored mail. Prewar newspapers were either shut down or printed only what the Germans allowed, and fewer people wanted to read them. Resistance papers began to publish very early. At first, some were produced on typewriters with a half-dozen copies passed from hand to hand. Later, they became more professional, sometimes secretly using the same printing presses as the legal newspapers. Eventually there were about 1,000 resistance newspapers in France and 300 in Belgium, with 12,000 people working on them. There were 315 papers in Denmark, which had only 4 million people. In the Netherlands, 120 newspapers were being published as early as 1941; there were another 150 within two years.

The official radio was also controlled, but people listened to Swiss radio or to the BBC (the British Broadcasting Corporation). It was the BBC that informed Europeans that Germany was losing battles and could be defeated. The Germans tried to prevent people from learning the truth. They wanted to keep people demoralized and unwilling to risk their lives, and their families' lives, in a cause that seemed hopeless. They levied heavy penalties on people caught listening to the BBC and, in 1943, even banned the ownership of private radios in the Netherlands altogether. Nonetheless, many people hid their radios and continued to listen in secret. To make up for the loss of radio news, some of the main Dutch resistance newspapers began publishing three times a week. The five largest papers had a combined circulation of 450,000.

Forced labor

German policy intentionally made jobs difficult to find in occupied areas because Germany had a labor shortage and wanted foreigners to work there. From the first days of the occupation, people in eastern Europe were sent to Germany and forced to work on farms and in factories. In parts of Poland, children as young as twelve were subjected to forced labor.

In western Europe, however, the Germans at first tried to persuade people to volunteer to work in Germany, promising high wages and good conditions. But they also made sure that some people would have little choice except to volunteer. An unemployed worker who refused to work in Germany, for example, would not receive unemployment insurance and could even have his or her ration card taken away—which could mean starvation. In France, the Germans promised to release French prisoners of war who had been captured in 1940 in exchange for Frenchmen who volunteered to work. For every six voluntary workers, the Germans did release about one prisoner of war, often the sickest individuals. By May 1941, about 45,000 French workers had gone to Germany, 33,000 of them from Paris, where unemployment was especially high.

The number of volunteers, however, was not enough. It became even lower as word came back that foreign workers in Germany were treated badly and were not making as much money as promised. So the Germans began drafting young men from western Europe to work in Germany. By the second half of 1942, 250,000 French workers had been sent to Germany by the *Service de Travaille Obligatoire* ("compulsory labor service"), or STO. Altogether, the STO drafted 641,000 Frenchmen, the largest number from any western country. The earlier volunteer workers were now treated the same as the STO workers: as prisoners. Counting French prisoners of war and some other categories, there were 1.7 million French workers in German industry in 1943. (For more information on forced labor in Germany, see Chapter 7.)

The STO and similar programs in other occupied countries had a result that the Germans had not anticipated. Most people in western Europe hated the Nazis and wanted the German occupation to end. But most, probably the great majority, were not ready to risk their freedom and their lives to oppose a seemingly all-powerful German army. They were waiting, hoping that Germany would lose the war and that they would be freed.

But now, young men faced a simple choice: report for forced labor in Germany or go into hiding. In France, thousands of men left home and hid in the forests and hills, where they joined the existing bands of resistance fighters. In the Netherlands, where the flat, treeless geography was not suited

But now, young men faced a simple choice: report for forced labor in Germany or go into hiding.

for guerrilla warfare, young men and women who hid from compulsory labor service were called *onderduikers,* or "divers." By the end of the war, there were an estimated 300,000 of them.

Hostages and retaliation

The growth of armed resistance as a result of the STO also led to an increase in civilian victims. Throughout occupied Europe, the Germans decided to shoot innocent civilians as revenge for acts of resistance. The high command of the German armed forces ordered all commanders to follow this policy. The idea was that if ordinary people were punished for things the resistance did, they would blame the resistance and would not support it. In general, the German policy did not work. As far as can be known, the people in occupied countries blamed the Germans, not the resistance, when the Germans murdered civilians. But, regardless of who was blamed, it did put many resistance organizations in the difficult position of causing the deaths of their fellow citizens. In some countries, most resistance organizations decided not to engage in attacks on the German occupying forces as a result of this policy.

Lidice erased

Often, German retaliation was intentionally far greater than the action of the resistance. In May 1942, a team of British-trained Czechoslovakian resistance fighters who had parachuted back into the country assassinated the high-ranking Nazi leader Reinhard Heydrich. The Germans retaliated immediately by killing at least 1,500 Czechs. A few days later, the Germans surrounded the coal-mining village of Lidice (LI-deet-su). Then they shot all 172 males over the age of sixteen. All the women and most children were sent to concentration camps. Very few of these children survived the war. A few of the Lidice children, who "looked German," were taken from their mothers and sent to German families instead. (The policy of seizing young children and "Germanizing" them without their parents' consent was also carried out in Poland and other parts of eastern Europe.) After killing or deporting all the people of Lidice, the Germans burned down every building in the town. Lidice was picked at random; it seems to have had no connection to the assassination of Heydrich.

Lidice became famous, and towns in America and other countries were renamed "Lidice" to show that the Nazis could never destroy it. But similar massacres happened throughout occupied Europe. In Norway in April 1942, the Germans burned down 300 houses in the town of Televaag, deported 75 people to concentration camps, and arrested another 260. The Dutch town of Putten was burned down and all its male citizens sent to concentration camps, where most of them died, in retaliation for a nearby attack that wounded one German.

French civilians punished

In Paris, people who were caught outside after the official curfew were arrested, held overnight, and usually released in the morning. But if German soldiers were killed during the night, then the curfew violators might be shot as a reprisal. In

German retaliation was intentionally far greater than the action of the resistance.

The Germans adopted a policy they called "Night and Fog" (Nacht und Nebel in German), under which the Nazis secretly took political opponents to concentration camps in Germany, where they disappeared—into the night and fog.

October 1941, the Germans shot fifty French civilians in the western city of Nantes in retaliation for the killing of one German officer. The Germans announced they would shoot fifty more hostages if the killers were not turned over to them within two days. The next day, after another German officer was killed in the southwestern city of Bordeaux, the Germans arrested one hundred people there and immediately shot fifty. The other fifty were held hostage, as in Nantes. But these actions created a tremendous outcry throughout the world and increased French hostility. The Germans decided not to shoot the fifty hostages in each city. But the general policy remained the same. By the end of the war, the Germans had executed 30,000 French hostages. In Greece, which had a much smaller population than France, the number of murdered hostages may have been as high as 45,000. In one Greek town, Klisura, 250 women and children were burned to death.

Captured resistance fighters, as opposed to civilian hostages, were often tortured to extract information and then hanged or shot. But, especially in western Europe, the Germans adopted a policy they called "Night and Fog" (*Nacht und Nebel* in German), under which the Nazis secretly took political opponents to concentration camps in Germany, where they disappeared—into the night and fog. There were no trials, no letters, no contact with the outside world. Families and friends would never know what happened, or whether the person was dead or alive. (In fact, a small number of "night and fog" deportees did survive the war in concentration camps.)

Protests, strikes, and sabotage

Resistance to German occupation often began early, but usually in nonviolent ways. People in the Netherlands waiting to cross the street would raise their hats when the light turned orange, which is the Dutch national color. Danish students wore knit caps in blue, white, and red so that they looked like the insignia on the planes of Britain's Royal Air Force. In many cities, everyone would stop talking whenever a German soldier entered a shop, and no one would say a word until he left.

From these kinds of actions, which were not very dangerous and had little effect on the Germans, some people moved on to larger, organized anti-German activities. Writing and distributing newspapers, as mentioned earlier in this chapter, were among the most important. But people found other ways to hurt the Germans. Workers producing products for Germany purposely did their jobs poorly, making sure that parts did not fit properly or that they would break after being used once. Clerks mislabeled shipments so that they were sent to the wrong place, causing delays. Even tardiness became a form of protest. In addition, more serious forms of sabotage (intentional destruction of military or industrial facilities) also became widespread.

Martial law declared

There were also more public forms of protest. On October 28, 1939, less than two months after the war began, university students in the Czech capital of Prague led large public demonstrations in honor of the Czechoslovakian national holiday. The demonstrations turned into battles with police, and the Germans retaliated by shutting down all Czech universities for the rest of the war.

In the Netherlands, students in Dutch universities staged a series of protests and strikes against the German order to remove all Jewish professors. In February 1941, another Dutch challenge to German anti-Jewish policy became one of the largest protests in occupied Europe. After an acid attack on German police in a Jewish-owned store, the Germans arrested 400 Jews off the streets of Amsterdam, the largest Dutch city, and sent them to a concentration camp. In protest, thousands of Dutch workers went on strike. They shut down public services, transportation, large factories, and the port of Amsterdam. As the strike spread to two nearby cities, the Germans declared martial law (military law, with many normal legal rights suspended) and sent large numbers of troops into the city to force people back to work. Strikers faced arrest and deportation to a concentration camp or even being shot on the spot.

In Denmark, which the Germans had treated less harshly than any other occupied country, there was a wave of strikes in 1943 to protest new German restrictions. The Germans declared martial law and disbanded the Danish government and army, both of which had been allowed to exist until then.

In most cases, the resistance was not just a war against the Germans. It was also against the people who supported the Germans during the occupation.

Some of the most significant strikes occurred in Italy in early 1943. At that time Italy was technically still an ally of Germany. (Chapter 10 describes the last days of Italy's alliance with Germany.) Beginning in the FIAT auto factories in the northern industrial city of Turin, the strikes spread to many industries in northern Italy. The workers demanded lower prices and better working conditions, but they also wanted Italy to get out of the war.

Armed resistance

Some form of armed resistance developed in almost every country Germany occupied. In a few places, such as Denmark and the Netherlands, the geographic conditions meant that these movements were confined to towns and cities and were therefore very small. Sometimes, the Germans succeeded in destroying much of the armed resistance movement, as they did in Czechoslovakia after the assassination of Reinhard Heydrich in May 1942. From then until the last days of the war, the remaining Czech resistance was made up of small groups that organized work slowdowns in factories and engaged in mostly small-scale sabotage.

In countries with deep forests or mountains, however, bands of resistance fighters, sometimes supplied with arms by parachute drops from Allied planes, began hit-and-run attacks against the occupiers. But in most cases, the resistance was not just a war against the Germans. It was also against the people who supported the Germans during the occupation, sometimes because they agreed with Nazi ideas and sometimes because they thought this was the way to get ahead. In other words, a European resistance movement often involved a civil war inside a country as well as a war between different countries.

The Slovak National Rising

This was true even in a German puppet state like Slovakia, a country the Germans had created when they took over Czechoslovakia in March 1939. A puppet state is a country that claims to be independent but is actually controlled by another stronger country. Slovakia's government was a dictatorship led by Father Josef Tiso, a Catholic priest who introduced Nazi-like policies. The Slovakian army attacked the Soviet Union alongside the Germans. By 1944, however, there was an underground guerrilla army, called partisans, operating in the countryside. Many Slovakian soldiers fighting in the Soviet Union had deserted and joined the Soviet army. Along with other Soviet agents, some of them parachuted back into Slovakia to help lead the partisans.

Then, in August 1944, much of the Slovakian army stationed at home launched a rebellion against Tiso and the Germans. The partisans joined this battle, which became known as the Slovak National Rising. Tiso's forces could not defeat the rebels, who soon controlled much of the country. The Soviets parachuted arms and supplies, and the Soviet army attempted to break through the German lines to reach Slovakia, but the German army stopped them. Then strong German reinforcements rushed into Slovakia to crush the National Rising. After heavy fighting, they defeated the rebels by the end of October. Tiso and the Germans then engaged in large-scale and bloody reprisals.

The armistice with Germany divided France into two parts. The German army occupied the northern half and all of the Atlantic coast. The southern part was controlled by the Vichy government.

France

One example of the way the war against Nazi Germany was also a civil war is France. France was considered the greatest military power in Europe when the war began. The speed and completeness of the German victory shocked the nation. (The defeat of France is described in Chapter 2.) The Germans placed a new French government in office, headed by Marshal Phillippe Pétain, a hero of World War I. Pétain had helped defeat the Germans in 1918, but now he was an old man of eighty-four. He believed the German victory in 1940 was a kind of punishment because the French people had failed to respect authority and had been allowed too much freedom before the war. As the historian Nora Levin has said, "More than Nazism, Pétain despised and feared democracy."

The armistice with Germany that stopped the fighting divided France into two parts. The German army occupied the northern half and all of the Atlantic coast. The southern part was controlled by Pétain's French government. Its laws also applied to the German-occupied zone if they did

Inside France, both in the occupied zone and in Vichy France, networks of resistance groups were born.

not interfere with German orders. France had to pay for the huge cost of the German occupation, millions of dollars a day, and Germany refused to release French soldiers taken prisoner in the battle.

Vichy France

The French government made its new capital at Vichy (pronounced VEE-she), a small city in central France. The constitution was changed to abolish democracy. Marshal Pétain was given dictatorial powers as the head of the new French State, which replaced the French Republic. Even the famous slogan of the republic, dating back to the French Revolution, was changed. Instead of "Liberty, Equality, Fraternity" (brotherhood), the Vichy government's slogan was "Work, Family, Country."

Some French people opposed Vichy from the beginning. Charles de Gaulle, a little-known army general, fled to London and declared that France should continue to fight Germany. With British support, he organized French forces that had escaped the country (soon called the Free French) to continue the war alongside the British. (De Gaulle and the Free French are described in Chapter 9.) Inside France, both in the occupied zone and in Vichy France, networks of resistance groups were born.

The reistance groups published illegal newspapers, hid people who the Nazis were trying to arrest, and tried to organize opposition to Vichy. Although they were often tiny at first, these groups eventually grew very large. They hid British and American airmen whose planes were shot down over France, attacked German troops, and blew up railroad lines.

But most French people were not active in the resistance, and certainly not at the beginning. A few pro-Nazi French were happy that Germany had defeated France. Others agreed with the Vichy government about what kind of country France should be, that democracy and freedom had gone too far. They supported a policy of cooperating with Germany.

Perhaps the largest number took a wait-and-see attitude. They respected Marshal Pétain and thought he would do his best for France in a difficult situation. They did not like the Germans who had conquered their country and did not share

the Nazis' ideas. But they wanted to continue to live their lives as best they could. They needed to earn a living and send their children to school. They hoped Vichy would be able to arrange for the release of the 2 million French prisoners of war held in Germany. They hoped Pétain could ease the harsh conditions the Germans were imposing on their country. Perhaps most of all, they hoped that for France the war was over.

This German gasoline supply train was derailed and burned by explosives placed in the tracks by French resistance firghters.
(Reproduced by permission of AP/Wide World Photos)

Collaboration

At the beginning of the occupation, when it looked almost certain that Germany would win the war, many French leaders thought that France's future—and their own personal power—depended on developing a close relationship with Germany. They wanted to collaborate with Germany. To collaborate means to work together, and the Vichy officials used the word to make it sound as if they were not simply obeying German orders. But the word soon took on a different meaning from what they had intended. Many French people could understand that France often had to do what Germany wanted. After all, millions of German soldiers were occupying France. But that was different from voluntarily collaborating. Many were outraged when the official newspapers published photographs of Marshal Pétain greeting German leader Adolf Hitler as a friend. Pierre Laval, the most powerful Vichy leader, openly said that he hoped Germany would win the war. As time went on, more and more people thought that Laval and his fellow collaborators were traitors to France.

Most of the things Germany wanted were very unpopular with the people of France. The Germans wanted money from the French government, they wanted to take over many French companies, and they wanted to buy French products cheaply. They wanted the crops grown on French farms. They wanted Vichy's cooperation in arresting and deporting all Jews from France. All of these things increased opposition to Vichy. When Vichy gave in to German demands and began drafting young Frenchmen for forced labor in Germany, many young men became active members of the resistance.

Pro-Nazi *Milice*

In response, Vichy created special pro-Nazi units of French volunteers, called the *Milice* ("Militia"), that worked with the SS, the military branch of the Nazi Party. Before long, the *Milice* and the resistance were fighting what amounted to an open civil war. When the Allied armies landed in France in June 1944 and drove the Germans out, the French resistance played an important part in destroying rail lines, guiding Allied troops, and slowing down the advance of German reinforcements. The greatest moment for the French resistance,

and perhaps for any resistance in occupied Europe, was the role it played in liberating Paris. (The Allied landing in France and the liberation of Paris are described in Chapter 11.)

Soviet Union

The largest armed resistance movement in Europe was the partisans of the Soviet Union. When the German tanks swept into the Soviet Union in June 1941 (see Chapter 3), they raced past large formations of Soviet troops. The advancing German infantry later captured many of these units, but other units remained free, regrouping in heavy forests and marshy areas that had few roads. Some of these free Soviet army units were still commanded by their regular officers and were prepared to continue fighting. Others consisted mainly of men who only wanted to get home. But getting home was often impossible without being captured. Word soon spread that the Germans killed most Soviet soldiers who surrendered.

French people who collaborated with the Nazis were subjected to humiliation after the war. These women's heads were shaved and then they were driven through the streets so everyone would know they had helped the Nazis. *(Reproduced by permission of the National Archives/USHMM Photo Archives)*

Soviet partisans

Trapped far behind the German army, the free Soviet units became the core of a guerrilla army, operating in groups of anywhere from 300 to 2,000 fighters. By the end of 1941, there were 30,000 of them. Soon they undertook thousands of small actions that interfered with the German invasion. Partisans cut telephone wires and blew up railroad tracks. They seized or burned German supplies, forcing the Germans to guard them more heavily. They also executed civilians who cooperated with the German occupiers.

The Soviet government immediately saw the value in partisan activity. By the autumn of 1941, it began training officers in guerrilla warfare. The graduates of these schools then parachuted behind German lines to join existing partisan units or create new ones. By the summer of 1942, there were 150,000 organized partisans; a year later, there were at least 200,000.

Germans welcomed at first

Not all partisans were Soviet soldiers trapped behind German lines. Many were local villagers who had joined the resistance. When the Germans first invaded the Soviet Union, some people welcomed them. This was especially true in Ukraine and the Baltic states of Estonia, Latvia, and Lithuania. Many of these people thought the Germans would free them from Russian domination. (Although the Soviet Union was made up of many nationalities, it was generally controlled by Russians, who were the largest group, and who had conquered these countries over the centuries.) The Communist government of the Soviet Union, which had come to power in 1922 and was led since 1924 by the brutal dictator Joseph Stalin, had treated the conquered peoples harshly.

Communism is a political and economic system based on government ownership of factories, banks, and most other businesses. During the 1930s in Ukraine, Stalin's secret police had executed many thousands of small farmers as they fought to keep their farms from being confiscated by the government. Hundreds of thousands of people had died in famines created by unwise and vengeful Soviet policies. Other opponents of the Communists were arrested and sent to Siberia, a frigid waste-

Thirteen year old Russian partisan.
(Reproduced by permission of AP/Wide World Photos)

land in the north of the country. It is then not surprising that many people in these areas were happy to see the Soviet army driven out and the Germans march in.

Townspeople join guerilla soldiers

Soon the way the Germans treated the local people turned most of them into enemies too. German officials treated the local populations with contempt, and took everything of value and sent it home. Tens of thousands of people were taken away to work as semi-slaves in Germany. The people left behind were treated just as badly; the Germans seized their crops and left them without enough to feed their families. Before long, support for the partisans grew dramatically. Large numbers of local people, including thousands of women, joined the partisan bands in the forests. Many thousands more cooperated with the partisans and provided them with information.

It is impossible to know how many German troops the Soviet partisans put out of action, and it is now clear that the claims made at the time were vastly exaggerated. But 35,000 is probably a fair estimate. Their military value went beyond wounding or killing German soldiers, however. The Russian partisans had the major advantage over other European resistance movements of working closely with a regular army that was near enough to support them: they could coordinate their activity with that of the Soviet army. For example, at the beginning of major Soviet offensives the partisans played an important role in limiting the German army's ability to transfer units by train from one part of the battlefront to another by destroying rail lines.

Yugoslavia

Aside from the Soviet Union, the most effective armed resistance movement in Europe was in Yugoslavia. As in France, the battle against the Germans was also partly a civil war between different groups inside the occupied country.

The invasion of Yugoslavia had been one of the German army's easiest victories. The million-man Yugoslav army surrendered in less than two weeks, and Germany and its partners,

known as the Axis, divided up the country. (See Chapter 3.) But this rapid success also meant that many Yugoslav army units were still intact when the country surrendered. Some officers immediately led their units into the hills to continue fighting. The most important leader was Draza Mihailovic, who had been deputy chief of staff of the Yugoslav Second Army. His band originally consisted of only fifty soldiers. As the movement grew, they became known as Chetniks, a name used by Serbs who had fought against the invading Turks in past centuries. Mihailovic and most top Yugoslav army officers were Serbs, the largest ethnic group in the country, and the one that had dominated Yugoslavia. The Chetniks were loyal to the Yugoslav king, who was from the Serbian royal family.

Croats and Serbs

But other ethnic groups in Yugoslavia had long resented Serbian control. The Croatians were the most prominent of

Most Serbian political parties refused to give in to any Croatian demands and tried to maintain Serbian domination of Yugoslavia.

these. Throughout the 1930s, various Croatian political parties struggled for greater Croatian rights within Yugoslavia, and some demanded complete independence. The most extreme of these groups was called the Ustashi ("rebel" in the Croatian language). It engaged in terrorist activities, including the assassination of Yugoslavia's king on a visit to France in 1934. The Ustashi took money from Benito Mussolini's Italy and modeled itself after Mussolini's Fascists and Adolf Hitler's Nazis, both militaristic organizations that brutalized their enemies. Meanwhile, most Serbian political parties refused to give in to any Croatian demands and tried to maintain Serbian domination of Yugoslavia.

Ustashi takes Croatia

During the Axis invasion of Yugoslavia, the Ustashi declared Croatian independence. The new independent Croatia was then protected by the German and Italian occupation forces and became an ally of Germany. The Ustashi government was one of the most vicious and murderous in all of Nazi-controlled Europe. Its troops engaged in horrible massacres of ethnic Serbs, Roma (gypsies), Muslims from Bosnia (another part of Yugoslavia), and Jews. In at least a few cases, even the Nazi SS, the military arm of the Nazi Party, complained about Ustashi brutality. At least 200,000 people, including Croatian opponents of the Ustashi, died at the Jasenovac concentration camp, where torture was common.

Germans take Serbia

In Serbia, the German military government was also among the most brutal in Europe. Although there was a puppet Serbian government, it was not important because, unlike the Ustashi government in Croatia, the Germans ran Serbia directly. The harshness of the occupation led to a rapid increase in the strength of Mihailovic's Chetniks. But the Chetniks had two key disadvantages. They wanted to return Yugoslavia to the way it was before the war, which meant continuing Serbian control of the country. That made it almost impossible for them to attract any anti-Ustashi Croatians, Slovenians, Bosnians, Montenegrins, or other ethnic groups of Yugoslavia. The second major Chetnik disadvantage was that they wanted to avoid fighting the Germans immediately. Instead, they wanted to gain more strength and wait until the Allied armies were nearby before beginning a major national uprising. One of the reasons for this policy was to avoid the savage reprisals against civilians that the Germans inflicted whenever there was armed resistance.

Tito leads Yugoslav Partisans

A second movement soon developed in Yugoslavia that did not have these disadvantages. This was the Partisans, led by Josip Broz, known as Tito, a leader of the Yugoslav Communist Party before the war. The Partisans said they wanted a new Yugoslavia, where each of the national groups would be treated equally and control its own area. Unlike the Chetniks, the Partisan leaders included non-Serbs, such as Tito himself, who was Croatian. Also, unlike the Chetniks, the Partisans had no plan to maintain aspects of the old Yugoslavia, where the great majority of people had been very poor. For Tito, the war against the Axis occupiers was also a revolution against the old system.

The Partisans had about 100,000 armed soldiers and were fighting the Axis in major operations. In a series of offensives, the Germans chased the Partisans from the mountains of Bosnia to Montenegro and back again, but they could not destroy them. Twenty thousand Partisans were killed or wounded in these campaigns. The Germans also slaughtered the local villagers even if they had not helped the Partisans.

Altogether, up to thirty Axis divisions—a significant number at more than 300,000 men—were needed in Yugoslavia because of Partisans' activity. Most of the Axis troops were Italian, with only a dozen German divisions. Few were first-rate combat units. The Partisans, on the other hand, received a tremendous amount of arms and equipment from the Italian troops in Croatia and other parts of Yugoslavia when Italy surrendered to the Allies in September 1943.

Another source of arms and supplies for the Partisans was the British and Americans. The British Special Operations Executive (SOE) and the American Office of Strategic Services (OSS) were in charge of gathering information and of sabotage in occupied Europe (see Chapter 15) and in aiding resistance

For Tito, the war against the Axis occupiers of Yugoslavia was also a revolution against the old system.

The fighting and killing in Yugoslavia was among the most savage of the war.

movements. At first the SOE and OSS favored the Chetniks because Mihailovic was the official representative of the pre-war Yugoslav government. But his reluctance to fight hurt his reputation with the British and Americans. Their opinion of him lessened even more when they began to believe that Mihailovic was more interested in destroying Tito and the Partisans than in fighting the Nazis and Italians. Indeed, the Chetniks even cooperated with the Axis forces in hunting down the Partisans.

Allies help Tito

Soon the British and Americans were supporting Tito, and by 1944 the British Balkan Air Force, based in Italy, was dropping large quantities of American arms and even sometimes supplying air support to the Partisans. Despite the fact that Tito was a communist and the British and Americans generally distrusted communist resistance movements, the Partisans were obviously willing and able to fight the Axis troops, while the Chetniks were not.

After the war it was learned that Tito also sometimes offered temporary truces to the Germans so that the Partisans could fight the Chetniks, but this was not well known at the time. The Chetniks and the Partisans knew they were fighting a civil war against each other while they were also fighting the Germans. The presence of the Ustashi in Croatia made it a three-way civil war. The rugged mountains made Yugoslavia well suited to guerrilla warfare. All these factors, plus the cruelty of the German occupation, ensured that the fighting and killing in Yugoslavia was among the most savage of the war. About 1.4 million people died—approximately one out of every ten.

The Holocaust

7

One of the things that made World War II different from other wars was that Nazi Germany was committed to goals that would lead to mass murder. The Nazi dictator Adolf Hitler had always had three goals. One was to destroy his opponents in Germany. A second was to make Germany the strongest country in Europe and to conquer *Lebensraum,* which means "room to live." This word implied that without this land, Germany could not survive: it was supposedly too small for its population. The third goal was to "purify" Germany—and then Europe—of "racial enemies" and to establish Germans as the "master race." These three goals were closely connected in Hitler's mind, and all three were mixed up with his hatred of Jews, which is known as anti-Semitism.

Official anti-Semitism

Even before the Nazis took over Germany, Hitler and other Nazi leaders had attacked the Jews in speeches, in newspapers, and in the slogans they shouted. They compared the Jews to germs that made healthy Germans sick, called them

Storm troopers in front of a Jewish-owned shop with a sign encouraging Germans to boycott the store.
(Reproduced by permission of the USHMM Photo Archives)

enemies of Germany, and demanded that they be thrown out of the country. For years, the brown-shirted storm troopers, the Nazi Party's military organization, had attacked and harassed Jews.

When the Nazis came to power, these anti-Semitic ideas became the official policy of the German government. The storm troopers stepped up their campaign of terror. They beat up Jews on the streets, attacked Jewish-owned stores, and forced Jews out of their jobs. Because the Nazis now ran the government, the Jews could not turn to the police for help. On April 1, 1933, only two months after Hitler became chancellor (head of the German government), the Nazis organized a national boycott of Jewish-owned stores.

Beginning in 1933, a series of laws denied Jews employment in many jobs, and many Jews decided that it was no longer possible to live in their own country. In 1933, 53,000 Jews left Germany—about one out of every ten Jews in the country. About 16,000 of them eventually returned, many because of the difficult conditions they faced as refugees (people who flee to another country to escape danger or mistreatment).

After the Nuremberg laws passed, the German government officially did not consider Jews to be citizens.

The Nuremberg laws

In September 1935, a special session of the Reichstag (the German national legislature) met in the southern city of Nuremberg. The Reichstag passed two laws, which had been written on Hitler's direct order. The first law said that only a person of "German or related blood" could be a citizen of Germany, and that only a citizen could have political rights or hold office. The second law made it illegal for Jews to marry or to have sexual relations with non-Jews.

Two months later, the Nazis issued a decree to carry out these laws. It said that anyone with three or more Jewish grandparents was a Jew. Anyone with two Jewish grandparents was a Jew if he or she "belonged to the Jewish religious community" or if he or she were married to a Jew.

The Nuremberg laws did several things. They put Jews into a special legal category, with fewer rights than other Germans. They said that Jews were not Germans, no matter how long their families had lived in the country or how loyal they had been. They said that being a German or a Jew was part of a person's "blood" and could never be changed. After the Nuremberg laws passed, the German government officially did not consider Jews to be citizens.

New laws and new violence

In 1938, the Nazis stepped up their attacks on German Jews. In March, a new law took away the right to own property or sign contracts from Jewish organizations such as synagogues (Jewish houses of worship). In April, all Jewish businesses, except the very smallest, were required to register with the government.

Early in June, the Great Synagogue of Munich was burned down. Later that month, the police arrested all German Jews with police records—which generally meant parking tickets. Fifteen hundred Jews were sent to concentration camps, brutal prison camps run by the SS, the elite Nazi military organization. During this time, the Nazis also went after Jews in Austria, which had become part of Germany in March. By September, 4,000 Austrian Jews were in concentration camps. The arrested Jews were released only if they agreed to leave the country. In August, the synagogue in Nuremberg was destroyed.

In October, the Gestapo (short for the German words for "secret government police") began rounding up Jews who were Polish citizens living in Germany to deport (forcibly remove) them to Poland. The Gestapo arrested 18,000 people, including whole families. On the night of October 27, the Gestapo put them on special trains and sent them to the Polish border. The Polish government refused to allow them into the country, however, and many were held in special camps on the border.

Crystal Night

Shortly afterward, Herschel Grynszpan, a seventeen-year-old Jewish man living in France, went to the German embassy in Paris and shot a German diplomat, Ernst vom Rath. Grynszpan's family was among those deported to Poland. The Nazis used this incident to claim that all Jews were at fault and that the shooting was a crime against all Germans.

On the night of November 9, 1938, word reached Germany that vom Rath had died of his wounds. The Nazis launched a nationwide campaign of planned mob violence. In every city in Germany, storm troopers wearing civilian clothing attacked Jewish homes, stores, synagogues, and orphanages, burning buildings and throwing furniture onto the street. The police did not interfere.

Seven thousand businesses were destroyed. The streets were filled with shards of the stores' windows, called *Kristall* in German. That gave the terrible night its name: *Kristallnacht,* or Crystal Night.

About a hundred Jews were killed, many beaten to death. Thousands of others were injured. An American diplomat in the city of Leipzig described how "an eighteen-year-old boy was hurled from a three-story window to land with both legs broken on a street littered with burning beds and other household furniture."

The same witness wrote that storm troopers threw terrified Jews into a stream after destroying their homes. Then the storm troopers ordered the spectators, ordinary Germans, to spit at the Jews and throw mud at them. The spectators, according to the American witness, were "horrified" by what was happening.

The violence was supposed to look like the "spontaneous" anger of the German people, not the work of the government or the Nazi Party. But no one was fooled. Nazi officials planned the attacks and storm troopers carried them out. Very few other Germans took part. Most Germans, as the American diplomat pointed out, were horrified by the violence, but almost no one tried to stop it.

Arrests and economic measures

Immediately after Crystal Night, 30,000 Jewish men were arrested and sent to concentration camps. They were gradually released on the condition that they and their families leave Germany within 30 days. Thousands of Jewish families had only days to make arrangements to leave their homeland.

The Nazis also used Crystal Night to destroy any ability Jews still had to earn a living in Germany. The German government decided to seize any insurance money paid to Jewish property owners. In addition, Jews were held responsible for repairing the damage caused by the storm troopers. Jewish-owned businesses that had been forced to close because of the

The violence of **Kristallnacht** *was supposed to look like the "spontaneous" anger of the German people, not the work of the government or the Nazi Party. But no one was fooled.*

destruction could not reopen unless they had non-Jewish owners. And the government "fined" the Jewish community 1 billion marks for vom Rath's death—an enormous amount.

On November 12, 1938, the government issued an official order entitled "Decree on Eliminating the Jews from German Economic Life." It prohibited Jews from selling any goods or services, from being independent craftsmen, or from being in the management of any company.

On November 15, the government expelled all remaining Jewish children from school. In December, Germany barred Jews from many public places, such as movie theaters and beaches.

After Germany had taken over Austria in March 1938, it applied the same anti-Jewish policies to that country. The same thing happened in the parts of Czechoslovakia that Germany seized in October 1938 and March 1939. But the condition of Jews in areas under German control became even worse after World War II began. The first victims were the Jews of Poland.

The first attacks on the Jews of Poland

The population of Poland before the war was about 35 million. About 3.3 million were Jews—almost one–tenth of the population. It was the largest and most important Jewish community in Europe, with a long and rich tradition.

A very large number of Jews, probably about 120,000, were killed during the weeks of fighting against the German invasion and immediately after. Jews in the Polish army, like all Polish soldiers, suffered heavy losses. Many Jewish civilians, like other Poles, died in German air raids. (The German invasion of Poland is described in Chapter 2.) But many other Jews were killed specifically because they were Jews.

Nazi brutality toward Polish Jews began immediately after the German occupation. (An occupation is when a country that has won a war stations military forces in the defeated country to control it.) Many of the worst incidents were committed by the *Waffen-SS* ("armed SS"). These were units of the SS, the military branch of the Nazi Party, that fought as part of the regular army. Worst of all was a special branch of the SS called the *Einsatzgruppen* ("special-action groups" or "special-

duty groups"). These specially trained strike forces were like a combination of army troops and secret police officers.

Humiliation and torture

The way the Nazis behaved reveals much about their hatred of the Jews. The Nazis were not just interested in getting rid of Jews who might be dangerous to them, as they were with

The Nazis destroyed synogogues in Germany and in the countries they conquered. Nearly all of Poland's synogogues were destroyed during the Nazi occupation. *(Reproduced by permission of the United States*

In the first six months of the German occupation, most of the synagogues of Poland were burned to the ground.

the Poles. They also wanted to humiliate and torture Jews as much as possible.

In the town of Bielsko on September 3, 1939, the Nazis forced 2,000 Jews into the courtyard of a Jewish school. The Nazis poured boiling water on some while they were hung by their hands; others died when their torturers forced water from a hose into their mouths until their stomachs burst. In Mielec, Nazis forced 35 Jews into a slaughterhouse and set it on fire, burning them alive.

In Wloclawek, the Nazis interrupted prayers in a private house on Yom Kippur (the Day of Atonement, the most sacred Jewish holiday). They ordered the people to go outside and run. Then they ordered them to halt. Five or six of the Jews did not hear this order, or did not halt quickly enough to suit the Nazis, and were shot dead.

The next day, the Nazis burned down the town's two synagogues, something they did all over Poland. In the first six months of the German occupation, most of the synagogues of Poland were burned to the ground.

German soldiers grabbed Jews on the streets and beat them. They cut off the beards that religious Jewish men always wore. They forced them to crawl through the mud, or to pull Germans around in carts, or to give the stiff-armed Hitler salute.

The Nazi plan for the Jews of Poland

On September 21, 1939, the deputy head of the SS, Reinhard Heydrich, sent a secret message to German authorities in Poland concerning "the Jewish question in the occupied territory." His first point was to remind the commanders of the *Einsatzgruppen* that the "final aim" of these actions was to be "kept *strictly secret.*" The final aim was not explained, but Heydrich said it "will require an extended period of time." However, he wanted to begin the first stages leading to this final aim immediately.

The first goal "should be to establish only a few cities" where the Jews would be concentrated (gathered), Heydrich wrote. To make later actions easier, the concentration points should all be at railroad centers, or at least on railroad lines. Once again, the later actions were not described, but the fact that the concentration points had to be convenient to railroad lines indicates that they were not intended as a final destination for the Jews.

Jews from small towns would be forced into the nearest city of concentration. These newcomers, like the Jews who already lived in the cities, would have to live in a special area of the city, separated by walls or fences. This was the beginning of the ghettos. In the Middle Ages, many European Jews were required to live in a special section of town, and usually had to return there by nightfall. In some places, including parts of Germany, these ghettos had lasted until the early nineteenth century. By the time of Heydrich's plan, however, Europe had been free of ghettos for many decades.

Reinhard Heydrich, deputy head of the SS. *(Reproduced by permission of AP/Wide World Photos)*

Heydrich also ordered the creation of a Jewish Council, usually called a *Judenrat,* in each Jewish community. Its members and their families would be held responsible for making sure the Jews followed German orders.

The beginning of the system of slave labor

After they occupied Poland, the Germans began using Polish Jews for slave labor. Jews were grabbed off the street and forced to do things like clear rubble from the recent battles or fill in antitank ditches that the Poles had dug.

On October 26, 1939, five weeks after Heydrich's message, an official decree gave the top SS leader in each area of occupied Poland authority over Jewish forced labor. Whenever some German agency needed some emergency work done, the SS formed a labor column of Jews they arrested at random on the street.

Within a few months, the Germans created more permanent labor camps. Soon, 30,000 Jews were digging an antitank ditch many miles long near the new border with the Soviet Union. Forty-five thousand others were held in 40 separate camps, building a canal near Lublin. Another 25,000 worked on a project near Warsaw. Non-Jewish Poles were also being sent to work camps.

Before long, Jews were performing forced labor in factories as well. Many German companies—including some owned by the SS itself—built factories next to the work camps. Some Nazi officials became rich by making deals with private businesses. Some of the Jews were paid about forty cents a day, but most were not paid at all. They worked under terrible conditions, without enough food, and the death rate was very high. Eventually a huge system of forced labor—or, really, slave labor—developed.

The first ghettos

At the same time as the forced-labor columns were being created, the Nazis moved ahead with Heydrich's plan to create ghettos. They collected the lists of Jews that each *Judenrat* had been ordered to draw up. Jews had to wear a yellow six-pointed star at all times and were not allowed to go into certain areas.

The Germans created the first ghetto in late October 1939, less than two months after Germany had invaded Poland. Several months later, a ghetto was established at Lodz, the second-largest city in Poland before the war. It took about another year for the Germans to set up ghettos throughout Poland. By April 1941, almost all Jews in Poland were confined in ghettos.

Although every ghetto was different, the conditions in Lodz give an idea of what they were like. The Nazis always chose the poorest section of town for the ghetto. The buildings were mostly old, run-down, and poorly heated in the cold Polish winters. Few had indoor bathrooms or running water. There were about 32,000 apartments inside the Lodz ghetto, most of them with only one room. On average, four people lived in every room. More than 160,000 people were jammed into an area of one-and-a-half square miles—about thirty city blocks.

In Warsaw, the capital of Poland and home to the largest Jewish population in Europe, around 450,000 Jews lived inside the walls of the ghetto. This was about 200,000 people for every square mile, almost triple the number for the rest of Warsaw, which was itself a crowded city. In the ghetto, an average of nine people lived in every room.

Hunger was the worst problem in the ghettos. Food in German-controlled Poland was rationed, so even people with

Beginning in late 1939, the Germans forced Polish Jews to move to certain areas of the city, always the poorest sections of towns, called ghettos. Many people died because of the poor living conditions. *(Reproduced by permission of Art Resource)*

money could legally buy only what the Germans allowed. Each person had ration coupons for different categories of food. Jews were not allowed to buy meat, poultry, fish, fruits, vegetables, eggs, or white flour. Their diet consisted mainly of potatoes and bread. Often they ate potato peels. Many Jews were so poor they could not even buy what the Germans allowed. The combination of cold, poor sanitation, overcrowding, and an inadequate diet led to disease and death. More than 43,000 people starved to death in the Warsaw ghetto in 1941, almost one-tenth of the population. At a funeral for some children from a ghetto orphanage, the remaining children placed a wreath on their graves. It read: "To the Children Who Have Died from Hunger—From the Children Who Are Hungry."

The invasion of Russia and the beginning of mass murder

While it was forcing the Jews of Poland into ghettos, Germany invaded the Soviet Union (Russia and the territory it controlled) on June 22, 1941. The Soviet army and government were completely unprepared. The German forces, led by tanks, pushed into Soviet territory with tremendous speed. (The German invasion is described in Chapter 3.) With them came four specially trained new *Einsatzgruppen.* They had been recruited from organizations of dedicated Nazis such as the Gestapo, the *Waffen-SS,* and the SD (from the German words for "security service," the special branch of the SS in charge of spying on the rest of the Nazi Party). These new *Einsatzgruppen* had received many lectures about Nazi ideas, including the need to exterminate "subhumans" such as Jews. They also received operational training in how to round up and kill large numbers of civilians. (Each *Einsatzgruppe* used the same procedures, even though they operated many hundreds of miles apart.) By the time their training was over, the officers and men of the *Einsatzgruppen* all knew that their job was to commit genocide, the deliberate, systematic destruction of a racial, national, or cultural group.

The shootings

As the German army advanced into Soviet territory, a subunit of an *Einsatzgruppe* swept into a town or village as soon

A member of *Einsatzgruppe D* prepares prepares to shoot a Ukrainian Jew. *(Reproduced by permission of the United States Holocaust Memorial Museum)*

as possible. One of their commanders later described what would happen. The Germans would "order the prominent Jewish citizens to call together all Jews for the purpose of resettlement." (Throughout Europe, the Germans told Jews that they were being "resettled" to some other area, when they were really being sent to their deaths.) When the town's Jewish population had gathered in some central location, such as a school or factory grounds, "they were requested to hand over their valuables to the leaders of the unit." Then the Germans marched them away, usually to a nearby forest. "The men, women, and children were led to a place of execution which in most cases was located next to an antitank ditch that had been made deeper." The Germans then told everyone to remove their outer clothing. (In many of the *Einsatzgruppen "aktions"* [operations], the victims had to remove all their clothing.) "Then they were shot, kneeling or standing, and the corpses thrown into the ditch." Afterward, an *Einsatzgruppe* officer would climb into the ditch full of dead bodies and shoot people who were still moving.

In other *Einsatzgruppen* operations, the Germans forced their victims to lie on their stomachs on the edge of a ditch, and a German standing directly over them would shoot them in the back of the neck with a rifle, which was supposed to be placed very close to the victim's neck. The victim's blood and brains often splattered the Germans' uniforms.

An SS colonel described how his unit killed Jews in a December 1941 report to his superiors. The unit would round up Jews from one or more towns and dig a ditch at the right site to hold the right number of bodies. "The marching distance from the collecting points to the ditches averaged about five kilometers [three miles]. The Jews were brought in groups of 500, separated by at least 2 kilometers [1.2 miles] to the place of execution."

Kovno

In the city of Kovno, in Lithuania (a country that had briefly been part of the Soviet Union), the murders began as soon as the Soviet army retreated from the city. Gangs of Lithuanian anti-Semites attacked and robbed Jews on June 23 and 24, 1941. On June 25, they marched from house to house in the Jewish slum district of the city, killing every Jew they could find. As they did in many other places, the Germans in Kovno encouraged these actions and secretly helped organize the mobs. It was important, the commander of an *Einsatzgruppe* wrote, to make it seem that the local population had attacked "the Bolshevist [Communist] and Jewish enemy on its own initiative and without instructions from the German authorities."

Ten thousand Jews from Kovno were arrested and taken to Fort Number Seven, one of several old military posts surrounding the city. For several days, large groups were taken out and shot; sometimes the Lithuanians raped the women first. Their bodies, almost 7,000 of them, were buried in large pits.

The Germans forced the 30,000 surviving Jews of the area to move to the slum district where the murder march had occurred. This became Kovno's ghetto. Throughout the summer of 1941, the Germans took hundreds of people from the ghetto and shot them. In October, more than 9,000 people, including thousands of children, were taken to Fort Number Nine and shot. The Germans called Fort Number Nine the *Schlachtfeld,* which means "slaughter ground." In the years that the Germans held Kovno, 100,000 people, 70,000 of them Jews, were killed in the forts surrounding the city.

The single worst massacre was at Kiev, the capital of Ukraine, which was then part of the Soviet Union. The German army captured Kiev on September 19, after a battle that lasted forty-five days. Within a few days, the Germans ordered all Jews to report for resettlement. They gathered, carrying small bundles, and were led out of town past the Jewish cemetery to an area of sand dunes, where there was a large ravine, a steep natural ditch. The name of the place was Babi Yar.

As each small group reached Babi Yar, the Germans ordered them to strip, hand over their bundles, and march to the edge of the great ravine. Then they were machine gunned. For two days the machine gunners worked and the bodies filled the ravine. Thirty-three thousand died.

The pattern was the same in every part of the Soviet Union captured by the Germans. The *Einsatzgruppen* would enter an area, round up as many Jews as they could, march them to an isolated area in the woods, and shoot them. Then the *Einsatzgruppen* would move farther east, following the advance of the German army. The surviving Jews were forced into ghettos and then killed in a series of roundups and executions. In five months, 500,000 Soviet Jews were dead.

The Wannsee Conference

At some point during this period, the top leaders of Nazi Germany decided to kill all the Jews in Europe. They

The pattern was the same in every part of the Soviet Union captured by the Germans. The **Einsatzgruppen** *would enter an area, round up as many Jews as they could, march them to an isolated area in the woods, and shoot them.*

called this the "final solution" to the Jewish "problem." They had already taken the first steps in this plan. The Jews of Poland were confined to ghettos, from which they could easily be taken elsewhere and killed. Soviet Jews had been murdered by the hundreds of thousands. In the other countries of Nazi-occupied Europe, Jews had to register with the police and wear a yellow star on their clothes at all times. The places where they could live were restricted.

On January 20, 1942, Heydrich called a conference at Wannsee, a lakeside suburb of Berlin. There, he informed representatives of each branch of the German government about the decision to kill the Jews and instructed them to cooperate in carrying it out. Heydrich told them that "evacuation of the Jews to the east" was now the policy of Nazi Germany. At this very moment, Heydrich said, "practical experience is being gathered that is of major significance in view of the coming Final Solution to the Jewish Question." The practical experience was being gained by the *Einsatzgruppen* in Russia.

Heydrich reported on the number of Jews in each country of Europe. The total was 11 million. Heydrich's figures included the Jews of Great Britain, which Germany was fighting. They also included countries that were not involved in the war, like Spain, Switzerland, and even Ireland. The aim of the final solution, in other words, was eventually to kill every Jew in all of Europe. The Nazis, according to their own figures, planned to kill 11 million people.

The fifteen men at the conference then discussed the problems involved in arresting the Jews of each country under German control or influence and deporting them to the east. The conference ended with discussions of exactly how best to kill the Jews. They described and debated the technical problems of mass shooting and using poison gas.

Deportations and death camps

On July 19, 1942, Heinrich Himmler, the head of the SS, ordered the resettlement of all Polish Jews by the end of the year. The Nazis began deporting Jews from the ghettos until no one was left and the ghetto was "liquidated." In the smaller ghettos, the entire population might be forced onto a single train. In the larger ghettos, the process took months. The Nazis would order a few thousand people to report to a central location and then put them on a train. They would never be seen again. Sometimes this went on day after day; sometimes there were long pauses. The trains were going to four special camps.

These camps were different from the older concentration camps in Germany. As terrible as the concentration camps were, the camps in Poland were something new. They were death camps or extermination camps. Four of the camps were built for the sole purpose of killing Jews. They were not meant to do anything else. None of the prisoners was put to work there, except to help run the killing process. Each trainload of Jews was killed as soon as possible.

These four camps killed more than 2 million Jews.

The first of these camps was Chelmno (Kulmhof in German), about 35 miles from Lodz. It began to operate in December 1941, even before the Wannsee Conference was held. People were brought to the nearest railroad station on trains and then driven to Chelmno in trucks. There the Nazis forced them into the back of a different truck that looked like a furniture van. The Nazis crammed as many people into each truck as could possibly fit and sealed the back so that no air could enter. They directed the exhaust from the truck engine into the back through a hose. When the engine of the truck was run, it sent poisonous carbon monoxide into the truck. The truck ran until all the people were dead. Then the Nazis drove the truck to the nearby forest and dumped the bodies into mass graves.

The Nazis repeated this procedure over and over. Three hundred forty thousand people died at Chelmno. All but 7,000 were Jews. Only three people survived.

The other three camps designed to kill the Jews of Poland were different from Chelmno but very similar to one another. Each was near a large center of Jewish population, but they were far enough away, hidden in the forests, so that their purpose could be kept secret. They were on railroad lines, so that the Jews from the Polish cities could be brought to them.

The first camp was Belzec, located between the cities of Lublin and Lvov. From February 1942 to the end of the year, 600,000 people died at Belzec. Almost all were Jews. Two people survived.

As terrible as the concentration camps were, the camps in Poland were something new. They were death camps or extermination camps.

The Nazis had approached the murder of Jews as a technical problem.

Sobibór was east of Lublin. From May 1942 until October 1943, 250,000 people died at Sobibór. Almost all were Jews. Sixty-four people survived.

Treblinka was near Warsaw. From July 1942 to August 1943, about 870,000 people were murdered at Treblinka. Almost all were Jews. Somewhere between forty and seventy people survived.

The three camps were designed so that they could kill people as quickly as possible. The Nazis had approached the murder of Jews as a technical problem. Each aspect of the killings was carefully thought out. They planned how to bring the Jews to the camps and how to deal with them when they arrived. They planned how to process them at the camps and exactly how to kill them, and they planned how to get rid of their clothes, their possessions, and, finally, their bodies.

The transports

The Jews who arrived at the camps had already suffered unbelievably harsh conditions on the transport trains that brought them to the camps. They arrived exhausted, starving, and desperate for water. Many had died on the trip. When the survivors were finally allowed off the trains, they were told they had reached a transit camp, a stop along the way to resettlement.

Among the descriptions of these transports, there are several written by officers of the German Reserve Police, who guarded many of the trains. The historian Christopher R. Browning quotes a report written by a Lieutenant Westermann.

Almost 5,000 Jews from Kolomyja in southeastern Poland who had reported for "registration" at 5:30 in the morning were loaded on a train to Belzec. The next day, Westermann wrote, "some 300 Jews—old and weak, ill, frail, and no longer transportable—were executed." It took until seven that evening to complete the loading of the train. "Each car of the transport was loaded with 100 Jews. The great heat prevailing that day made the entire operation very difficult," Westermann reported. The cars were sealed and their doors nailed shut, as usual, he explained. But because it was already dark by the time the train left at nine, and because of the great heat,

"many Jews escaped by squeezing through the airholes after removing the barbed wire. While the guard was able to shoot many of them immediately, most of the escaping Jews were eliminated that night or the next day by the railroad guard or other police units." In a different transport to Belzec, 2,000 of the Jews had died from suffocation or heat prostration before the train arrived.

Transport to a death camp.
(Reproduced by permission of the United States Holocaust Memorial Museum)

Arrival

When the transport trains reached the death camps, the Nazis brought the first twenty freight cars to the unloading area, while the others waited farther away. The camps were surrounded by barbed wire fences, with high watchtowers at the corners. There were tree branches and leaves in the fencing so that no one could see through.

A group of prisoners opened the doors and the guards ordered all the Jews out. (The prisoners who opened the doors

In a few minutes, all evidence of what had happened on the train was erased.

were men, usually young and healthy, who had arrived on an earlier transport and had not been killed.) The SS men and the guards (often Ukrainian soldiers in the Soviet army who had been captured by the Germans and who had volunteered to help the Nazis) marched the new arrivals into the camp as quickly as possible. Anyone who lagged behind was beaten with rifle butts or whipped.

Meanwhile, the prisoners who had opened the cars removed the bodies of those who had died on the train. Then they cleaned the cars. They washed away blood, vomit, and human waste and swept out bits of clothing or personal possessions left behind. In a few minutes, all evidence of what had happened on the train was erased.

The guards told the people who had just gotten off the train to leave all their belongings. Then they separated the men from the women and children.

The women and children were forced to run to a long barracks building and told to undress completely so that they could be disinfected in the shower houses. The women would then have their hair cut off, to prevent disease, they were told. The hair, in fact, was used to make products for the German armed forces, such as water-resistant rope for the navy.

Next, the women and children were forced by the guards to run, completely naked, through a narrow path between barbed wire fences. Like the fence outside the camp, they were camouflaged with tree branches to prevent anyone seeing through. The path, about a hundred yards long, was called the "tube."

The guards beat and whipped the women and children to make them run through the tube before they could realize what was happening. There was a sign that said "To the showers," but the path really led to a secret part of the camp where the killing took place.

While the women were being processed, the men waited. They too were naked. After a while, perhaps half an hour or more, they too were forced to run through the tube.

On the other side of the path was a building. It looked like a public bathhouse, which was a familiar sight in Europe in that period. As they came through the tube, the prisoners were forced to enter the building through the main door. Inside there were doors to smaller rooms, where showerheads hung from the ceiling. These rooms also had doors to the outside of the building, but these were sealed.

The guards packed the Jews into these rooms as tightly as possible and then sealed the rooms. Then they turned on the engine of a captured Russian tank. The carbon monoxide gas from the engine pumped through the showerheads into the sealed rooms, which were really gas chambers. For half an hour the poisonous gas poured in. The people inside gasped and coughed and choked. They clawed desperately to escape. Their bodies were drenched with sweat, with blood, with their own waste. They did not even have room to fall down when they died. They died pressed against one another, their bodies tangled together.

The money, gold, jewelry, and other valuables that the Jews had handed over in return for a receipt were now the property of the Nazis.

Disposal

After all the prisoners were dead, a special group of the permanent prisoners opened the outside doors to the gas chambers. They had to separate the bodies and remove them. Other prisoners washed out the gas chambers to make them ready for the next victims.

Meanwhile, other prisoners, known as the "dentists," searched the mouths of the dead for gold teeth and fillings and removed them with pliers. Then prisoners carried the bodies to several giant pits located about 150 to 200 yards from the gas chambers, threw them in, and buried them. The next group of victims would be thrown on top of them.

The permanent prisoners also sorted through all the belongings of the victims. All identification had to be removed. The yellow stars that the Nazis had ordered the Jews to wear were ripped off the clothing. The names were taken off their suitcases. The Nazis were sending the belongings of the dead to Germany. No one was to know where they came from. Huge mounds of clothing and shoes were piled in a large, open area. The money, gold, jewelry, and other valuables that the Jews had handed over in return for a receipt were now the property of the Nazis.

Women sort through a pile of shoes that had belonged to inmates killed at Auschwitz.
(Reproduced by permission of the United States Holocaust Memorial Museum)

The Nazis burned their identification papers, passports, birth certificates, photographs, and letters. They wanted no trace of their victims to survive.

Meanwhile, the next twenty cars of the train, which had been parked farther away, were brought to the camp. The whole process was now repeated.

Auschwitz

The most infamous death camp was Auschwitz, in southwestern Poland. Unlike the camps designed to kill the Polish Jews, Auschwitz was also an immense slave-labor camp, designed to hold more than 200,000 prisoners at one time, including many non-Jews. It was much bigger than the other camps, with hundreds of buildings. But its main purpose was not slave labor. Auschwitz was designed to kill Jews from all over Europe, not just Poland, although 300,000 Polish Jews died there. Transports came to Auschwitz for two and a half years, from France, Holland, Hungary, Norway, Italy, Greece, Belgium, and Slovakia.

These Jews had been arrested in their home countries, rounded up by the German occupation authorities or, in some countries, by the police of their own country, who were helping the Nazis. Usually they had been sent to a transit camp in their own countries until transportation became available. Like Jews everywhere, they had been told they were being resettled somewhere in the east. The terrified prisoners had often spent many days locked in the boxcars.

The railroad tracks went right into the camp. As each transport was unloaded, SS doctors "selected" the new arrivals. A small minority, especially adult men under the age of forty who appeared healthy, were told to go to the right. They would become slave laborers, trying to survive in some of the worst conditions ever endured by human beings. Some of those selected were chosen so that Nazi doctors could use them for horrible medical experiments.

Most of the people, perhaps 90 percent, were sent to the left: children and almost all women, anyone who appeared sick or weak, and all old people. Being sent to the left meant immediate death in the gas chambers.

Auschwitz had more and larger gas chambers than the other camps. Each of the chambers was connected to crematoria, special furnaces where the victims' bodies were burned. There was no need to bury the bodies in giant pits. The brick smokestacks of the crematoria stood high above the camp, like a factory. The smoke that rose from these chimneys for month after month was the symbol of a giant factory of death: the lives of more than 1 million human beings ended at Auschwitz.

The smoke that rose from these chimneys for month after month was the symbol of a giant factory of death: the lives of more than 1 million human beings ended at Auschwitz.

The Impact of Total War   8

World War II was larger than previous wars and was fought in more parts of the world. But it was different in another way, too. It came closer than any prior conflict to being a total war. It was not fought just by soldiers and sailors. Instead, each country tried to use all its resources to support the war. Victory in World War II depended, more than anything else, on supplying armies with huge quantities of industrial products. A country needed modern weapons, including planes, bombs, tanks, submarines, aircraft carriers, and machine guns. It needed the ships, railroads, and trucks to transport them; the fuel to run them; and the grease to lubricate them. It needed enough boots, uniforms, and helmets for its soldiers. The people who built these products, as well as the scientists and engineers who developed new weapons (see Chapter 15) and the writers and filmmakers who waged psychological warfare (see Chapter 16), were as important to the war effort as the soldiers in the armies.

If all the people of a country were involved in the war, then the country could ask the civilian population to make major sacrifices to win the war. And if the civilian population

The Staple Inn in London, dating from the sixteenth century, was destroyed during a German bombing raid. *(Reproduced by permission of the Corbis Corporation [Bellevue])*

were necessary for victory, then they were also targets for the enemy. If World War II were a war of the people, then the people were its victims as well as its fighters. (The impact of World War II in the United States are described in Chapter 5; some of the experiences of civilians in Europe are described in Chapter 6; and the German attempt to destroy the Jewish people, known as the Holocaust, is described in Chapter 7.)

Death from the air

One of the ways in which the war was brought home to civilian populations was by attacks from the air. In the first days of the war, the German air force (the Luftwaffe) heavily bombed Warsaw, the Polish capital. Then the Luftwaffe destroyed the center of the Dutch port of Rotterdam in May 1940. In both places, many civilians were killed and injured, and there was heavy damage to nonmilitary structures such as homes, schools, and hospitals. Shortly after, when large numbers of civilians clogged the roads of Belgium and France trying to escape the advancing Germans, Luftwaffe planes sometimes swooped down and fired machine guns at them to increase their panic and to block the movement of the Allied armies. (These events are described in Chapter 2.)

Although they caused civilian deaths, the air attacks were closely connected to efforts by German ground troops to capture the cities they were bombing or to cut off enemy forces. The Luftwaffe had been fashioned to work closely with the tanks and foot soldiers of the army. It had no four-engine heavy bombers, large planes that can travel long distances carrying heavy loads of bombs. Because the Germans based their military planning on the belief that the war would be short, they did not think they would need the Luftwaffe to operate independently of the German ground troops.

The RAF and the strategic air offensive

The German military strategy was in sharp contrast to that of Britain's Royal Air Force, the RAF (pronounced are-ay-eff). Formed in 1918 at the end of World War I, the RAF was the first air force that was not part of the army or navy. In contrast, the American air force was still part of the army until after World War II. Because the RAF was an independent service, it looked for an independent part to play in a war.

The RAF developed the idea of the strategic air offensive, a direct, long-term bombing attack on the enemy's homeland to destroy the enemy's means or will to continue the war. One way to do this is by bombing the factories that build the enemy's weapons. Bombers can also attack other enemy industries vital to the war effort, such as steel mills, coal mines, and dams needed to provide electric power to factories and oil refineries needed to provide fuel for planes and tanks.

Supporters of the strategic air offensive theory believed it might even bring victory by itself, rather than just helping the army win. They were certain that, at the very least, it would cause Germany to collapse much sooner, and with the loss of far fewer British lives. The RAF's predictions about the effects of bombing were partly based on the belief that it was impossible

RAF gunners in full kit with oxygen masks, parachutes, and guns. *(Reproduced by permission of the Corbis Corporation [Bellevue])*

to defend against bombing; that, in the words of former British leader Stanley Baldwin, "the bomber will always get through."

British planners also had a wildly exaggerated idea of how much damage German bombing of Britain would cause. A secret study predicted that the Luftwaffe could drop an average of 700 tons of explosives on Britain every day. The study expected that each ton would kill or injure 50 people. This would amount to 35,000 people per day—2 million in the first two months of war—a rate Britain could not endure. The study expected that three-quarters of the 7 million citizens of London, Britain's capital, would have to be evacuated and that between 3 and 4 million people in Britain would suffer mental breakdowns because of the bombing in the first six months.

No loss of life such as this happened. The actual number of British people killed or injured by German bombs in the entire war was about the number predicted for the war's first week. The 60,000 civilians who died was a very high number, but it was nowhere near enough to make Britain give up.

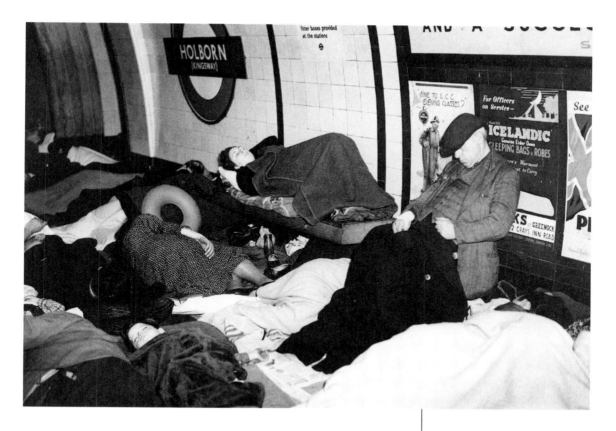

The Battle of Britain

The idea that bombers could not be stopped was first proved wrong by the RAF itself. In the summer of 1940, the Luftwaffe began an extended series of air attacks on England that became known as the Battle of Britain. Although not designed for strategic bombing, the Luftwaffe was sent on an ongoing mission to fight and destroy the RAF's fighter planes because Germany could not invade England until it had crushed the RAF. Soon, there was a second purpose for the German air raids: to make the British people feel that there was no chance to win the war and so force Britain to make peace without a German invasion. (The background and events of the Battle of Britain are described in Chapter 2.)

Because of the fear of British retaliation against German cities, the Luftwaffe at first limited its attacks to military or semimilitary targets. The first German attack on London was an accident, and it did not come until August 24, six weeks after the beginning of the campaign. The British retaliated by

Londoners take shelter from an air raid in a subway station. *(Reproduced by permission of the Corbis Corporation [Bellevue])*

bombing German cities. So, beginning on September 7, the Luftwaffe began massive attacks on London. Although these attacks were aimed at military targets such as the docks along the Thames River, there was heavy damage and loss of life in residential and commercial neighborhoods.

The fighter pilots of the RAF shot down so many German planes that by the middle of September it became clear that Germany had lost the Battle of Britain. It would not be able to invade England. The Luftwaffe shifted to night raids on London and other British cities in October and November 1940 and continued for months. Because night bombing was so inaccurate at that time, the raids were not really an attempt to hit military targets or factories. They were meant to cause as much damage and loss of life as possible.

Bombing blind

Strategic bombing in World War II was certain to cause many civilian deaths. Even if the bombing were accurate, it would kill many workers in the targeted factories and mines. In fact, the way strategic bombing was carried out made it very inaccurate. In built-up cities, many of the bombs aimed at factories or shipyards hit the residential areas surrounding them.

Strategic bombing was inaccurate for a number of reasons. There were no computers to measure factors like the plane's speed, direction, and altitude, as well as wind velocity, to determine the exact moment to release the bombs. Pilots and bombardiers had to calculate these factors, use their eyes, and rely on their experience to try to time the release accurately. Clouds and smoke made targeting even more complicated. Additionally, the bombers had to fly at high altitudes to avoid antiaircraft fire from the ground, and the need to dodge enemy ground fire and fighter planes made it difficult to keep a steady course.

Heavy losses

The number of planes lost in bombing raids was very high, especially at first. To attack cities in Germany, the RAF had to fly long distances over German-controlled Europe. On

both legs of the round-trip, Luftwaffe fighter planes attacked them. The deeper into Germany they went, the worse their losses were. Because British fighter planes did not have the fuel capacity to fly as far as the bombers, the bombers could not be escorted all the way to their targets. In a raid on Berlin, Germany's capital, in November 1941, 12.5 percent of the bombers were shot down. At that rate, a bomber—and its crew—would last an average of only eight missions, much faster than they could be replaced. Any losses over 5 percent meant that the Luftwaffe would eventually wipe out the British bomber force. The fighter pilots of the Luftwaffe, like the RAF's fighter pilots in the Battle of Britain, proved that bombers could be stopped.

Because of these factors, the British soon stopped daylight bombing missions. After the first few months of the war, the RAF flew strategic bombing missions only at night. Especially in the first years of the war, this meant the bombs were released blind. Because of the blackout, the pilots and navigators could not see any electric lights from their target cities.

An RAF crew checks in after returning safely from a bombing raid. Air raids into Germany generally suffered heavy losses. *(Reproduced by permission of the Corbis Corporation [Bellevue])*

Of the 600,000 German civilians killed in bombing raids during the war, about 120,000 were children.

During blackouts, cities would require that all lights, street-lights, car lights, even flashlights could not be used outside after dark. People had to put heavy black curtains in their windows so that light would not show outside the house. The pilots and navigators relied on navigational charts, moonlight, or the fires caused by earlier bombs. Then they reported on how successful they thought they had been. However, after the RAF began taking photographs of bomb damage, it became clear that the crews' reports were unreliable and that the bombers were doing a very poor job of hitting their targets.

At one point, a British study found that only 10 percent of the planes dropped their bombs within five miles of the intended target. Even when technical developments such as new versions of radar increased accuracy tremendously, only a small proportion of bombs landed closer than the length of two or three football fields from their targets.

"Area" or "terror" bombing?

The RAF chiefs realized that the only target they could count on hitting was an entire town. If the strategic air offensive were to continue, it needed a different justification than destroying factories. On February 14, 1942, Bomber Command, the RAF branch in charge of strategic bombing, issued a directive that the "primary object" of the campaign was to destroy "the morale [spirit] of the enemy civilian population and in particular of industrial workers." The head of the RAF explained that the target was residential areas, "not, for instance, the dockyards or aircraft factories." The aim was to kill the people who worked in the factories, along with their families, and to destroy their homes. In fact, of the 600,000 German civilians killed in bombing raids during the war, about 120,000 were children. The tactic was called "area bombing," but B. H. Liddell Hart, a leading British military historian, described it as a policy of "terrorization."

In March 1942, the RAF attacked Lübeck and then Rostock, two small cities on the Baltic seacoast of northern Germany. The centers of both historic cities, dating from the Middle Ages, were completely destroyed by incendiary (fire-starting) bombs. The factory areas outside the central districts suffered little damage. The Luftwaffe retaliated by bomb-

Arthur "Bomber" Harris

A week after the RAF adopted the strategic air offensive directive, Air Marshal Arthur Harris, soon known as "Bomber" Harris, became head of Bomber Command. He was a firm believer in the new policy. Harris argued that long-term bombing attacks that would destroy the enemy's industrial resources and demoralize its population was the only correct use of bombers. He opposed the use of bombers in any other operations. Indeed, he even tried to prevent the temporary interruption of the strategic air offensive in spring 1944, when the British transferred the bombers to France, where they were needed to attack railroads and bridges before the Allies could invade Normandy. With bombed-out roads, the Germans would be prevented from bringing reinforcements to the invasion beaches. Harris claimed that bombers were not suited for this job, and General Dwight D. Eisenhower, the supreme Allied commander, had to threaten to resign before Harris would give in.

Air Marshal Arthur Harris, known as "Bomber" Harris. (*Reproduced by permission of the Corbis Corporation [Bellevue]*)

Military experts and historians agree that the campaign Harris opposed so strongly was probably the most successful air campaign of the war and perhaps the bombers' most important contribution to the Allied victory in Europe.

ing historic and militarily unimportant towns in England, including Bath and Canterbury.

In May 1942, the RAF launched the first of its "1,000" raids. The first target was Cologne, Germany's third largest city. One thousand bombers caused fires that destroyed 600 acres in the middle of the city, with only 40 bombers shot down. From March to July 1942, the RAF dropped 58,000 tons of bombs in a series of attacks on cities in the Ruhr, Germany's

The great cathedral is almost the only undamaged building in the center of Cologne following an attack by one thousand British bombers in May 1942. The fact that the cathedral survived was probably just luck. *(Reproduced by permission of AP/Wide World Photos)*

most important industrial area, a campaign the RAF called the Battle of the Ruhr.

Firestorm

In late July, a large RAF force attacked the great seaport of Hamburg with incendiary bombs on four straight nights. For a combination of reasons, including the weather, the way Hamburg was built, and the fact that the raids destroyed the city's water pipes, the attacks resulted in a new and terrible event: a firestorm.

Hamburg burned continuously from July 24 to July 30, until 62,000 acres were destroyed. The fire created winds reaching tornado speeds, which were sucked into the center of the fire area. There, temperatures rose to 1,500 degrees Fahrenheit, and anything that could burn burst into flames—including people. Those in underground bomb shelters suffocated as

the fire drew in all the oxygen. Eighty percent of the buildings in Germany's second-largest city were damaged or destroyed. At least 30,000 people died, including about 6,000 children. Similar firestorms were created in several other cities. In some smaller cities like Magdeburg, where 9,000 died, the proportion of deaths was much higher than in Hamburg.

The RAF launched sixteen major raids on Berlin from November 1943 to March 1944. Until then, despite four years of war, life in Berlin had gone on normally, although 1 million of its 4.5 million inhabitants had been evacuated as a precaution. Because Berlin was a more modern city than Hamburg, with solidly built buildings and wide avenues and open plazas that prevented fires from spreading, there were no firestorms. An extensive system of well-designed bomb shelters kept the number of deaths down. But the physical destruction was still vast. About 1.5 million people were made homeless by the raids.

In February 1945, the RAF and the American air force attacked the city of Dresden in three short raids. Considered

Destruction in Hamburg after an RAF atack.
(Reproduced by permission of the Corbis Corporation [Bellevue])

one of the most beautiful cities in Europe, Dresden was almost undamaged until then because it had little military importance. But that also meant it was almost undefended by the Luftwaffe or antiaircraft guns. The city was jammed with German refugees (people fleeing from danger) who were trying to escape the advancing Soviet armies farther east. A total of 1,223 Allied planes caused a firestorm, like the one in Hamburg, that wiped out the city and killed a large number of civilians. Because so many people had recently arrived in the city, it is impossible to know the exact number of deaths; estimates range from 30,000 to 135,000.

Morality and effectiveness

The horror of the Dresden raid, coming as a time when it was certain that the Allies would win the war, made even many who had supported area bombing uneasy, including Winston Churchill, who was prime minister (head of the government) of Britain through almost the entire war. Even before Dresden, critics had argued that area bombing amounted to the intentional slaughter of civilians and was something the Allies should not do, even if the Nazis did.

In addition, the effectiveness of area bombing was doubtful. Even though the amount of bombs dropped on Germany rose from 48,000 tons in 1942 to more than 210,000 the following year and more than 900,000 in 1944, Germany produced 28,000 fighter planes in 1944, more than five times as many as in 1942. It produced three times as many tanks. Part of the reason was that the Germans had begun scattering their factories, breaking up large plants and relocating them to other areas. The new sites were unknown to the Allies, often disguised as something else, and sometimes built underground.

Even after the great Hamburg firestorm, industrial production in the city returned to about 80 percent of its pre-raid level within a few months. There is no indication that the people of Hamburg, or any other German city, were driven to rebel against the Nazi government, which supposedly was one of the goals of area bombing. In fact, the Nazis used area bombing to help convince average Germans that the British—not the Nazis—were barbarians who made war against defenseless children.

The cost of area bombing was high. Bomber Command lost 55,000 men in the campaign against Germany, most of them highly trained pilots, navigators, and bombardiers. Many more were shot down and became prisoners. These men, and the resources used to build the planes they flew and the bombs they dropped, might have made more of a difference if used in other ways.

The strategic air offensive, at least at first, was popular with the British people because for a long time it was the only way Britain could strike at Germany. The same was true for people in the German-occupied countries of Europe. It also forced the Germans to use about 2 million people, who were needed elsewhere, as part of the antiaircraft effort on the ground, and forced the Luftwaffe to devote many of its fighter planes to defend German cities, rather than fight the Soviet armies. Some historians believe this was its major contribution to the war. Almost all question whether the gain, however, justified the killing of so many civilians.

The Nazis used area bombing to help convince average Germans that the British—not the Nazis—were barbarians who made war against defenseless children.

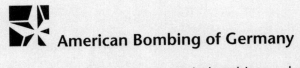

American Bombing of Germany

The American strategic bombing campaign against Germany generally avoided area bombing. (The United States did use area bombing against Japan, described in Chapter 14.) Instead, the American air force, concentrated on hitting specific industrial targets. The targets were chosen after economic experts analyzed which factories were most needed and would be the most difficult to replace. For example, the Americans attacked a plant that was one of Germany's few sources of ball bearings, which are needed in all motor vehicles. But sites like these were strongly defended, and the American daylight raids suffered heavy losses, just as Air Marshal Arthur Harris and the Royal Air Force predicted.

The most important target for the Americans became Germany's production of gasoline and aviation fuel. Germany had few sources of petroleum and increasingly relied on synthetic (chemically produced) fuel made from coal and other sources. The plants that produced fuel could not be broken up into smaller units and were difficult to hide. The campaign against the synthetic oil plants eventually became tremendously successful, but only after the introduction of a new American plane, the P-51 Mustang. This was the first fighter that had the fuel capacity to accompany the bombers all the way to their targets and protect them against German attack. The shortage of fuel, especially aviation fuel, was a key factor in the final collapse of the German armies.

Another major American target was the transportation system, which was more important than ever because the big factories were scattered around Germany. In fact, the collapse of German industry in 1945 was probably caused by the destruction of the transportation system, rather than because the industries themselves had been bombed. But by the time this collapse occurred, Allied ground troops were pouring through Germany, so it is impossible to know what part the bombing itself played.

Poison gas: The weapon that was not used

When the war began, one of the greatest fears—both of governments and ordinary people—was that the enemy would use poison gas. Both sides had used this weapon on the battlefield in World War I, killing thousands of soldiers and causing many others to suffer painful and sometimes deadly after-effects for many years. Hitler himself had been injured in a gas attack while fighting in the German army in 1918, at the end of World War I.

The greatest danger was that planes would drop poison gas bombs onto cities in air raids. The British issued millions of gas masks to civilians, including specially designed masks for infants. But Germany did not drop poison gas on London, or anywhere else, and it did not fire gas-filled artillery shells on the battlefield. Neither did any other country. Each was afraid that the other side would then do the same, and the Allies publicly announced that they would use poison gas against Germany if the Germans used it first. But there were some close calls.

Each of the major countries produced poison gas weapons and sometimes even shipped them to the battlefront, to be ready in case the enemy used them. In fact, in December 1943, 1,000 Allied soldiers and Italian civilians were killed when a German air raid blew up an American ship carrying poison gas bombs in the port of Bari in southern Italy.

The Germans actually tested poison gas, including new forms of deadly nerve gas, using captured Soviet soldiers and concentration camp prisoners as guinea pigs. (Concentration camps were the brutal prison camps where the Nazis sent their enemies.) Japan apparently used poison gas in China before World War II and continued testing it on prisoners once the war began.

In the summer of 1940, when everyone thought Germany would soon invade England, Churchill approved a plan to use poison gas against German attackers who got beyond the beaches. Four years later, when Germany began attacking Britain with V-1 "flying bombs" and V-2 rockets, Churchill wanted to use gas on Germany in retaliation. (The German "V-weapons" are described in Chapter 15.) He dropped the idea because his generals opposed it, as did American President Franklin D. Roosevelt. American military men wanted to use poison gas once in a battlefield situation—to force Japanese soldiers out of their underground hiding places during the battle of Iwo Jima. (See Chapter 14.) Roosevelt said no.

The greatest danger was that planes would drop poison gas bombs onto cities in air raids.

Soviet partisans. About 200,000 women joined the troops fighting behind German lines. *(Reproduced by permission of the Corbis Corporation [Bellevue])*

Women and total war

In the past, war had mostly affected young men. In World War II, other sections of the population were involved more than ever before. One of the great changes was in the expanded role of women.

Soviet Union

In a few cases, this expanded role meant taking a role in direct combat, especially in the Soviet Union. In the first few months of the German invasion, 1 million Soviet soldiers were killed and another 3 million captured. With such a severe short-age of manpower, Soviet women were recruited not only to do things like dig antitank ditches but also to join combat units.

Although they were still the exception, Soviet women drove tanks and flew planes in combat. One all-woman squadron flew their outdated planes on ten missions a night to bomb German troops during the Battle of Stalingrad. The Germans called them the "night witches." The most famous woman ace of the war was Soviet fighter pilot Lily Litvak, "the rose of Stalingrad," who shot down twelve German planes before she was killed in combat. In all, about 800,000 women served with the regular Soviet armed forces, although most did not see combat. Another 200,000 were partisans, troops operating behind German lines, employing hit-and-run tactics. (Partisans are described in Chapter 6.)

Great Britain

In most countries, women's roles in the armed services were limited to noncombat positions. In Britain, nearly half a million women served in the various women's branches of the armed forces or the nursing corps. Four hundred thousand were involved in defending against German air attacks, including operating antiaircraft guns during air raids. In theory, women were not allowed to fire the guns themselves, but they did everything else, such as operating searchlights and radar sets. Women—including Princess Elizabeth, who later became Queen Elizabeth II— drove trucks and ambulances. There were also more than a million part-time members of the Women's Voluntary Service (WAS), who did things like provide tea to soldiers passing through their towns or darn soldiers' socks, saving valuable material.

In December 1941 in Britain, single women between twenty and thirty years old became subject to the military draft, though they could choose to enter civil defense and similar work instead of the armed forces. By the end of the war,

Russian women snipers. Soviet women served in combat roles during World War II, including flying fighter planes and driving tanks. *(Reproduced by permission of the Corbis Corporation [Bellevue])*

Nurses served on the front lines all over the world.
(Reproduced by permission of the Corbis Corporation [Bellevue])

125,000 women had been drafted into the women's branches of the armed services.

United States

Although large numbers of women were serving in the armed forces in Britain, it took several months after the United States entered the war for the U.S. Congress to authorize the establishment of a Women's Auxiliary Army Corps, or WAAC on May 15, 1946. A year later, the WAAC became a full-fledged branch of the army called the Women's Army Corps, or WAC. Women's navy and marine corps forces were established in 1943. A total of 350,000 women were members of the armed services during the war. As in most countries, women were not permitted to serve in any combat roles. The WACs would free up more men for combat by filling important non-combat jobs. About half the women performed office work. Others worked in such diverse jobs as weather observer and forecaster, cryptographer (working with codes and secret communications), radio operator, photographer, and map analyst. Although some top officers strongly encouraged recruiting women to replace men in noncombat army jobs, others were hostile to the idea.

The Women's Airforce Service Pilots, or WASPs, received a great deal of publicity during the war—even having a movie made about the group. Between 1942 and 1944, more than 1,000 women served as pilots in the WASPs, flying a total of 60 million miles. One of their main jobs was flying planes from the factories where they were assembled and the airfields where they were tested to ports for overseas shipment by boat. They flew every American military plane, including the huge B-29 Superfortress. Near the end of the war, they even flew the experimental jet fighters.

Poster encouraging women to join the armed services.
(Reproduced by permission of the National Archives and Records Administration)

The women were responsible for testing various aspects of the aircraft they flew, such as their ability to jam enemy radar or to swoop low and attack ground targets with machine guns. The WASPs also towed targets that were used for practice by fighter pilots and antiaircraft gunners. The planes flown by the women were often hit since live ammunition was used in these exercises. Although the commander of the Army Air Corps strongly supported the WASPs, many other Air Corps officers resented their presence. Pilots thought of themselves as the elite of the military, and many found it disturbing that women could fly planes as well as men.

Children and total war

British children were also impacted by the war in a dramatic way. When the war began, British experts were sure that German air raids on London and other English cities would kill hundreds of thousands of people a week. They also expected the Germans to drop bombs containing poison gas. Because of

Rationing, Recycling, and Fellowship

Rationing and recycling were facts of life in Britian during World War II. Nothing was wasted, and anything that could be recycled was recycled: even potato peels were saved to feed to pigs. The government limited the clothing styles that could be manufactured. To save material, men's pants could not have cuffs, and women's skirts were made shorter. Clothing was severely rationed, and buying new wearing apparel was extremely rare. Children wore hand-me-downs. New shoes for civilians, including children, were unavailable: leather was reserved for soldiers' boots. People were allowed to buy new furniture only if their house had been bombed. Only one pattern of dishware was produced.

Tea and fresh eggs were difficult to get. Oranges and other imported fresh fruit almost disappeared. So did chocolate. Even ordinary food like butter and meat were rationed. People did not eat as much and had less variety in their diets.

There were other inconveniences, too. The blackout, in which all lights had to be off at night, made it hard to go anywhere after dark. In many places, street signs and road names were removed to delay the Germans if they invaded, but this only confused residents.

Although the shortages and rationing were inconvenient, many British people viewed the wartime atmosphere in a positive way. They liked the feeling that the whole country was working together for a common goal. Everyone seemed to belong to one of the numerous volunteer organizations. Many were air raid wardens, who made sure people got into shelters, which many families built in their backyard. In London, thousands of people went into the subway stations during air raids. Everywhere posters urged people not to repeat any information they learned because German spies were supposedly everywhere ("Loose Lips Sink Ships" was the most famous slogan). Other posters showed Prime Minister Winston Churchill with a defiant look on his face. Many people remember that England seemed much friendlier in those years. There were fewer trains, so they were more crowded—but strangers traveling together now spoke to each other instead of reading their newspapers. In the cities, the crowded air raid shelters became neighborhood meeting places.

these fears, in September 1939, at the very beginning of the war, more than 800,000 children were evacuated—without their parents—from London and other large cities and sent to small towns or villages in the countryside. Half a million mothers of preschoolers, with their children, were also evacuated.

Although many children were evacuated from London during the war, some stayed. This child was wounded during the German blitz. *(Reproduced by permission of AP/Wide World Photos)*

Most returned within a few months, during the period known as the phony war, when there were no German attacks on Britain. (This period is described in Chapter 2.) When German air attacks began again, many again left London. The same thing happened in 1944, when the V-weapon attacks began. (See Chapter 15.) Apart from physical dangers and shortages, one of the most dramatic effects of the war on children in countries such as Britain and the United States was the way it disrupted normal

A Child's View of the War

In 1940, when she was five years old, Ann Stalcup watched the German bombers overhead, on their way to attack the city of Bristol in western England, less than 20 miles from her home in the small town of Lydney. She heard the explosions and saw the flames' reflection on the river that passed her town.

In 1943, German prisoners of war were put to work on some farms near Lydney. Stalcup remembers that when they first arrived, they had only bloody rags to wear until the local people found old clothes for them. "No one blamed the soldiers for the war. The war was Hitler's fault. I was only eight but I was sure of that."

ways of growing up. An English child who was eight when the war began was fourteen when it finally ended—and probably could no longer remember a time before the war. Soldiers might be separated from their families for years, and no one could be sure if they would ever come back. Every child knew a friend whose father or older brother or uncle was killed in the war.

Victims and orphans

Children in countries conquered by the Nazis suffered much more. The clearest example was the Holocaust, the Nazis' attempt from 1941 to 1945 to kill all the Jews of Europe. (Chapter 7 describes the Holocaust.) Even before the war, Jewish children in Germany suffered constant discrimination. They were expelled from schools and attacked by Nazi thugs. Many Jewish families left Germany, but fleeing became increasingly difficult. In the last ten months before the war, German Jewish parents, who were unable to leave themselves, sent about 9,000 of their children to Britain. They traveled through Europe on special trains called *kindertransporte* ("children's transports"). Although separated from their parents, friends, and homeland, these children were the lucky ones.

The overwhelming majority of Jewish children in German-controlled Europe, perhaps 85 percent, were murdered during the war—a much higher rate than adults. In extermination camps such as Auschwitz, designed to kill thousands of people a day, healthy adults might be spared and used as slave labor, but children were killed immediately. In addition, in the ghettos, the walled-in Jewish sections of towns that the Germans established in eastern Europe, there was starvation and constant epidemics of diseases caused by malnutrition, exhaustion, and inadequate sanitation. Children, especially very young children, were more likely to die from these

causes than adults. Children were also less likely to survive by hiding in forests or escaping over mountains. Something like 1.5 million Jewish children died in the Holocaust.

Even so, many thousands of Jewish children survived the war, usually by being hidden by non-Jewish families or by Christian churches, even though their parents had died. But they were not the only children left alone. There were 1 million orphans in Poland at the end of the war and tens of thousands in France. One of every eight children in Greece was without parents. In 1945, when Germany surrendered, more than 10 million children in Europe had—at least temporarily—been abandoned or lost by their parents.

Germany: Fanatics and rebels

For years, the Nazis had heavily pressured young people in Germany to join official Nazi organizations like the

London children waiting to be evacuated. Most returned to their families in London after a few months. *(Reproduced by permission of the Corbis Corporation [Bellevue])*

Hitler Youth and the League of German Girls. By 1939, membership was legally required. These groups sponsored sporting events and similar social activities. But they also taught young Germans Nazi ideas, gave the youths uniforms, and marched them in Nazi parades. Older boys received military training, and many entered the army. In 1944, an entire armored division, called the Hitler Youth Division, was formed entirely from young men who had just "graduated" from the Hitler Youth. It fought with great courage and determination, but it was also the unit that murdered captured Canadian soldiers during the Battle of Normandy. (See Chapter 11.) In other words, the Hitler Youth had trained these young men to be fanatical Nazis.

Not all German young people participated in official Nazi groups, despite the law. In fact, some wanted to stay out so much that they became rebels against the Nazi government. In some of the big cities, especially in the Rhineland region of western Germany, loose groups of unskilled workers—usually between fourteen and eighteen years old—formed. They had various names, but the best-known groups were called Edelweiss Pirates. The edelweiss is a white flower that grows high in the Alps, the great mountain range of western Europe, and the Pirates wore one, or sometimes a white pin, hidden under the left lapel of their coats.

Originally, many of the Edelweiss Pirates just wanted to hike or go camping without Nazi interference. Soon, however, they began mocking Hitler and the Nazis in songs and in the graffiti they scrawled on walls. They attacked members of the Hitler Youth on the streets and tried to assassinate local Nazi officials. Sometimes they engaged in industrial sabotage, intentionally destroying machines or products.

The government considered the Pirates criminal street gangs, and, in some ways, some of them were. But their targets, and the things they wrote and said, made it clear that they hated everything the Nazis stood for. Because of this, the Gestapo (the Nazi secret police), whose job was to crush enemies of the government, hunted them. Although twelve Pirates were publicly hanged, without trial, in Cologne in 1944, the Gestapo never succeeded in destroying them entirely.

Where to Learn More

The following list of resources focuses on material appropriate for middle school or high school students. The list is divided into sections, separating general sources from those that cover specific aspects of World War II; certain titles are applicable to more than one subject area and are repeated under different headings. Please note that web site addresses, though verified prior to publication, are subject to change.

General Sources:

Awesome Library. *World War II.* [Online] http://www. awesomelibrary.org/ Classroom/Social_Studies/ History/World_War_II.html (accessed on August 13, 1999).

Canadian Forces College. "Military History: World War II (1939-1945)." *War, Peace and Security Guide.* [Online] http://www.cfcsc.dnd.ca/links/ milhist/ (accessed on August 13, 1999).

Clancey, Patrick. *Hyperwar: A Hypertext History of the Second World War.* [Online] http://metalab.unc.edu/ hyperwar (accessed on August 13, 1999).

Freeman, Michael, and Tim Mason, eds. *Atlas of Nazi Germany.* New York: Macmillan, 1987.

Graff, Stewart. *The Story of World War II*. New York: E. P. Dutton, 1978.

Krull, Kathleen. *V is for Victory*. New York: Knopf, 1995.

Lawson, Don. *Great Air Battles: World War I and II*. New York: Lothrop, Lee & Shepard Co., 1968.

Marrin, Albert, *The Airmen's War: World War II in the Sky*. New York; Atheneum, 1982.

National Archives and Records Administration. *A People at War*. [Online] http://www.nara.gov/exhall/people/people.html (accessed on August 13, 1999).

Reynoldson, Floria. *Women and War*. New York: Thomson Learning, 1993.

Ross, Stewart. *Propaganda*. New York: Thomson Learning, 1993.

Snyder, Louis L. *World War II*. New York: Franklin Watts, 1981.

Sullivan, George. *The Day Pearl Harbor Was Bombed: A Photo History of World War II*. New York: Scholastic, 1991.

Yale Law School. "World War II: Documents." *The Avalon Project at Yale Law School: Documents in Law, History, and Diplomacy*. [Online] http://www.yale.edu/lawweb/avalon/wwii/wwii.htm (accessed on August 12, 1999).

Young, Peter. *Atlas of the Second World War*. New York: Berkley Windhover, 1974.

Asia and the Pacific:

Blassingame, Wyatt. *The U.S. Frogmen of World War II*. New York: Random House, 1964.

Castello, Edmund L. *Midway: Battle for the Pacific*. New York: Random House, 1968.

Conroy, Robert. *The Battle of Bataan: America's Greatest Defeat*. New York: Macmillan, 1969.

Dolan, Edward F. *America in World War II: 1942*. Brookfield, Conn.: Millbrook Press, 1991.

Dolan, Edward F. *America in World War II: 1943*. Brookfield, Conn.: Millbrook Press, 1992.

Grant, R.G. *Hiroshima and Nagasaki*. Austin: Raintree, Steck-Vaughn, 1988.

Harris, Nathaniel. *Pearl Harbor*. N. Pomfret, Vt.: Dryad Press, 1986

Marrin, Albert. *Victory in the Pacific*. New York: Atheneum, 1983.

Morin, Isobel V. *Days of Judgment*. Brookfield, Conn.: Millbrook Press, 1995.

Nicholson, Dorinda. *Pearl Harbor Child: A Child's View of Pearl Harbor—from Attack to Peace*. Honolulu: Arizona Memorial Museum Assn., 1993.

Rich, Earle. *The Attack on Pearl Harbor*. San Diego: Lucent, 1998.

Sauvrain, Philip. *Midway*. New York: New Discovery Books, 1993.

Sherrow, Victoria. *Hiroshima*. New York: New Discovery Books, 1994.

Skipper, G.C. *Battle of Leyte Gulf.* Chicago: Children's Press, 1981.

Skipper, G.C. *Submarines in the Pacific.* Chicago: Children's Press, 1980.

Stein, R. Conrad. *The Battle of Guadalcanal.* Chicago: Children's Press, 1983.

Stein, R. Conrad. *The Battle of Okinawa.* Chicago: Children's Press, 1985.

Stein, R. Conrad. *Fall of Singapore.* Chicago: Children's Press, 1982.

Stein, R. Conrad. *Hiroshima.* Chicago: Children's Press, 1982.

Taylor, Theodore. *The Battle off Midway Island.* New York: Avon Books, 1981.

See also: Japan

Europe, the Atlantic, and Africa, 1939-43:

Blanco, Richard L. *Rommel, the Desert Warrior: The Afrika Korps in World War II.* New York: J. Mesmer, 1982.

Barnett, Correlli Barnett. *The Battle of El Alamein; Decision in the Desert.* New York: Macmillan, 1964.

Hoobler, Dorothy, and Thomas Hoobler. *Joseph Stalin.* New York: Chelsea House, 1985.

Humble, Richard. *U-Boat.* New York: Franklin Watts, 1990.

Kronenwetter, Michael. *Cities at War: London.* New York: New Discovery Books, 1992.

Marrin, Albert. *Stalin.* New York: Viking Kestrel 1988.

Reynolds, Quentin James. *The Battle of Britain.* New York: Random House, 1953.

Severance, John B. *Winston Churchill: Soldier, Statesman, Artist.* New York: Clarion Books, 1996.

Skipper, G.C. *The Battle of the Atlantic.* Chicago: Children's Press, 1981.

Skipper, G.C. *The Battle of Britain.* Chicago: Children's Press, 1980.

Skipper, G.C. *Battle of Stalingrad.* Chicago: Children's Press, 1981.

Skipper, G.C. *Fall of the Fox, Rommel,* Chicago: Children's Press, 1980.

Skipper, G.C. *Goering and the Luftwaffe.* Chicago: Children's Press, 1980.

Skipper, G.C. *Invasion of Sicily.* Chicago: Children's Press, 1981.

Sloan, Frank. *Bismark!* New York: Franklin Watts, 1991.

Stein, R. Conrad. *Dunkirk.* Chicago: Children's Press, 1982.

Stein, R. Conrad. *Invasion of Russia.* Chicago: Children's Press, 1985.

Stein, R. Conrad. *Siege of Leningrad.* Chicago: Children's Press, 1983.

Taylor, Theodore. *Battle of the Arctic Seas: The Story of Convoy PQ 17.* New York: Crowell, 1976.

Whitelaw, Nancy. *Joseph Stalin; from Peasant to Premier,* New York: Dillon Press, 1992.

Germany:

Ayer, Eleanor. *Adolf Hitler.* San Diego: Lucent, 1996.

Ayer, Eleanor. *Cities at War: Berlin.* New York: New Discovery Books, 1992.

Berman, Russell A. *Paul von Hindenburg.* New York: Chelsea House, 1987.

Eimerl, Sarel. *Hitler Over Europe; The Road to World War II.* Boston: Little, Brown, 1972.

Emmerich, Elizabeth. *My Childhood in Nazi Germany.* New York: Bookwright, 1991.

Friedman, Ina R., *The Other Victims: First-Person Stories of Non-Jews Persecuted by the Nazis.* Boston: Houghton Mifflin, 1990.

Fuller, Barbara. *Germany* New York: Marshall Cavendish, 1996.

Goldston, Robert C. *The Life and Death of Nazi Germany.* Indianapolis: Bobbs-Merrill, 1967.

Heyes, Eileen. *Adolf Hitler.* Brookfield, CT: Millbrook Press, 1994.

Heyes, Eileen. *Children of the Swastika: The Hitler Youth.* Brookfield, CT: Millbrook Press, 1993.

Marrin, Albert. *Hitler.* New York: Viking, 1987.

Nevelle, Peter. *Life in the Third Reich: World War II.* North Pomfret, VT: Batsford, 1992.

Shirer, William L. *The Rise and Fall of Adolf Hitler.* New York: Random House, 1961.

Spence, William. *Germany Then and Now.* New York: Franklin Watts, 1994.

Stein, R. Conrad. *Hitler Youth.* Chicago: Children's Press, 1985.

Steward, Gail B. *Hitler's Reich.* San Diego: Lucent Books, 1994.

Tames, Richard. *Nazi Germany.* North Pomfret, VT: Batsford, 1992.

Wepman, Dennis. *Adolf Hitler.* New York: Chelsea House, 1989.

Williamson, David. *The Third Reich.* New York: Bookwright Press, 1989.

Italy and Fascism:

Crisp, Peter. *The Rise of Fascism.* New York: Bookwright, 1991.

Hartenian, Lawrence R. *Benito Mussolini.* New York: Chelsea House, 1988.

Leeds, Christopher. *Italy Under Mussolini.* New York: Putnam, 1972.

Lyttle, Richard. *Il Duce: The Rise and Fall of Benito Mussolini.* New York: Atheneum, 1987.

Japan:

Behr, Edward. *Hirohito: Beyond the Myth.* New York: Villard Books, 1989.

Black, Wallace B., and Jean F. Blashfield, *Hiroshima and the Atomic Bomb.* New York: Crestwood House, 1993.

Grant, R.G. *Hiroshima and Nagasaki.* Austin: Raintree, Steck-Vaughn, 1988.

Hoobler, Dorothy, and Thomas Hoobler *Showa; The Age of Hirohito.* New York: Walker & Co., 1990.

Severns, Karen. *Hirohito*. New York: Chelsea House, 1988.

Sherrow, Victoria. *Hiroshima*. New York: New Discovery Nooks, 1994.

Stein, R. Conrad. *Hiroshima*. Chicago: Children's Press, 1982.

The United States:

Brimner, Larry Dane. *Voices form the Camps*. New York: Franklin Watts, 1994.

Cannon, Marian. *Dwight David Eisenhower: War Hero and President*. New York: Franklin Watts, 1990.

Coleman, Penny. *Rosie the Riveter; Women Workers on the Home Front in World War II*. New York: Crown, 1995.

Darby, Jean. *Douglas MacArthur*. Minneapolis, MN: Lerner, 1989.

Devaney, John. *Franklin Delano Roosevelt, President*. New York: Walker and Co., 1987.

Dolan, Edward F. *America in World War II: 1942*. Brookfield, CT: Millbrook Press, 1991.

Dolan, Edward F. *America in World War II: 1943*. Brookfield, CT.: Millbrook Press, 1992.

Duden, Jane. *1940s*. New York: Crestwood, 1989.

Freedman, Russell. *Franklin Delano Roosevelt*. New York: Clarion Books, 1990.

Hacker, Jeffrey H. *Franklin D. Roosevelt*. New York: Franklin Watts, 1983.

Harris, Jacqueline L. *The Tuskegee Airmen: Black Heroes of World War II*. Parsippany, NJ: Dillon Press, 1995.

Levine, Ellen. *A Fence Away From Freedom*. New York: G.P. Putnam, 1995.

McKissack, Pat. *Red-tail Angels: the Story of the Tuskegee Airmen of World War II*. New York: Walker & Co., 1995.

O'Connor, Barbara. *The Soldier's Voice: The Story of Ernie Pyle*. Minneapolis, MN: Cardrhoda Books, 1996.

Oleksy, Walter. *Military Leaders of World War II*. New York: Facts on File, 1994.

Pfeifer, Kathryn Browne. *The 761st Tank Battalion*. New York: Henry Holt, 1994.

Sinott, Susan. *Doing Our Part: American Women on the Home Front During World War II*. New York: Franklin Watts, 1995.

Spies, Karen Bornemamm. *Franklin D. Roosevelt*. Springfield, NJ: Enslow Pub. Inc., 1999.

Stanley, Jerry. *I Am an American*. New York: Crown, 1994.

Stein, R. Conrad. *The Home Front*. Chicago: Children's Press, 1986.

Stein, R. Conrad. *Nisei Regiment*. Chicago: Children's Press, 1985.

Sweeney, James B. *Famous Aviators of World War II*. New York: Franklin Watts, 1987.

Tunnell, Michael O., and George W. Chilcoat, *The Children of Topaz*. New York: Holiday House, 1996.

Uchida, Yoshika. *Desert Exile; The Uprooting of a Japanese-Ameri-*

can Family. Seattle: University of
Washington Press, 1982.

Whitman, Sylvia. Uncle Sam Wants You: Military Men and Women in World War II. Minneapolis, MN: Lerner Publications Co., 1993.

Whitman, Sylvia. V is for Victory. Minneapolis, MN: Lerner Publications Co., 1993.

Wings Across America. WASP on the Web. [Online] http://www.wasp.wwii.org (accessed on August 12, 1999).

Woodrow, Martin. The World War II GI. New York, Franklin Watts, 1986.

Zeinert, Karen, Those Incredible Women of World War II. Brookfield, CT: Millbrook Press, 1994.

Children in the war:

Asscher-Pinkoff, Clara. Star Children. Detroit: Wayne State University Press, 1986.

Besson, Jean-Louis. October `45: Childhood Memories of the War. Mankato, MN: Creative Editions, 1995.

Butterworth, Emma Macalik. As the Waltz Was Ending. New York: Four Winds, 1982.

Cross, Robin. Children and War. New York: Thomson Learning, 1994.

Drucker, Olga Levy. Kindertransport. New York: Henry Holt, 1992.

Foreman, Michael. War Boy: A Country Childhood. New York: Arcade, 1990. (England)

Gelman, Charles. Do Not Go Gentle: A Memoir of Jewish Resistance in Poland 1941-1945. North Haven, CT: Archon Books, 1989.

Holliday, Laurel. Children in the Holocaust and World War II. New York: Pocket Books, 1995.

Isaacman, Clara. Clara's Story. Philadelphia: Jewish Publication Society, 1984.

Marx, Trish. Echoes of World War II. Minneapolis, MN: Lerner, 1994.

Roth-Hano, Renée. Touch Wood: A Girlhood in Occupied France. Portland, OR: Four Winds Press, 1988.

Stalcup, Ann. On the Home Front; Growing Up in Wartime England. North Haven, CT.: Linnet Books, 1998.

Ungerer, Tomi. A Childhood Under the Nazis. Niwot, CO: Tomic, 1998.

Wassiljewa, Tatjana. Hostage to War. New York: Scholastic Press, 1997.

Wojciechowska, Maia. Till the Break of Day. New York, Harcourt, Brace Jovanovitch, 1972.

Events in Europe, 1944 and later:

Banfield, Susan. Charles de Gaulle. New York: Chelsea House, 1985.

Black, Wallace B. Battle of the Bulge. New York: Crestwood House, 1993.

Black, Wallace B. Victory in Europe. New York: Crestwood House, 1993

Bliven, Bruce. *The Story of D-Day: June 6, 1944*. New York: Random House, 1956.

Dolan, Edward F. *The Fall of Hitler's Germany*. New York: Franklin Watts, 1988.

Hine, Al. *D-Day: The Invasion of Europe*. New York: American Heritage Publishing Co., 1962.

Marrin, Albert. *Overlord: D-Day and the Invasion of Europe*. New York: Atheneum, 1982.

Morin, Isobel V. *Days of Judgment*. Brookfield, Conn.: Millbrook Press, 1995.

Rice, Earle. *The Nuremberg Trials*. San Diego: Lucent Books, 1997.

Skipper, G.C. *Death of Hitler*. Chicago: Children's Press, 1980.

Skipper, G.C. *Mussolini: A Dictator Dies*. Chicago: Children's Press, 1981.

Stein, R. Conrad. *The Story of D-Day*. Chicago: Children's Press, 1977.

Stein, R. Conrad. *World War II in Europe: America Goes to War*. Hillside NJ: Enslow Press, 1984.

Whitelaw, Nancy. *A Biography of General Charles de Gaulle*. New York: Dillon Press, 1991.

The Holocaust:

Arad, Yithak. *The Pictorial History of the Holocaust* New York: Macmillan, 1992.

Bachrach, Susan D. *Tell Them We Remember: The Story of the Holocaust*. Boston: Little, Brown, 1994.

Chaikin, Miriam. *A Nightmare in History: The Holocaust, 1933-1945*. New York: Clarion Books, 1987.

Feldman, George. *Understanding the Holocaust*. Detroit: UXL, 1998.

Frank, Anne. *The Diary of Anne Frank: The Definitive Edition*. New York, Bantam Books, 1997.

"The Holocaust." *The Jewish Student Online Research Center (JSOURCE)*. [Online] http://www.us-israel.org/jsource/holo.html (accessed on August 13, 1999).

Meltzer, Milton. *Never to Forget*. New York: Harper & Row, 1976.

Museum of Tolerance Online Multimedia Learning Center. *Auschwitz-Birkenau*. [Online] http://motlc.wiesenthal.org/pages/t003/t00315. (accessed on August 12, 1999).

Resnick, Abraham, *The Holocaust*. San Diego: Lucent Books, 1991.

Rogasky, Barbara. *Smoke and Ashes*. New York: Holiday House, 1988.

Rossel, Seymour. *The Holocaust: The Fire that Raged*. New York: Frank;in Watts, 1989.

Strahinich, Helen. *The Holocaust: Understanding and Remembering,* Springfield, NJ: Enslow, 1996.

United States Holocust Memorial Museum. *The Holocaust: A Learning Site for Students*. [Online] http://www.ushmm.org/outreach/nrule. (accessed on August 13, 1999).

Resistance

Bauer, Yehuda. *They Chose Life; Jewish Resistance in The Holocaust.* New York: American Jewish Committee, 1973.

Friedman, Ina R. *Flying Against the Wind: The Story of a Young Woman Who Defied the Nazis.* Brookline, MA: Lodge Pole Press, 1995.

Healey, Tim. *Secret Armies; Resistance Groups in World War II.* London: Macdonald, 1981.

Landau, Elaine.*The Warsaw Ghetto Uprising.* New York: Macmillan, 1992.

Pettit, Jayne. *A Time to Fight Back: True Stories of Wartime Resistance.* Boston: Houghton, Mifflin, 1996.

Stadtler, Ben. *The Holocaust: A History of Courage and Resistance.* West Orange, NJ: Behrman House, 1974.

Stein, R. Conrad. *Resistance Movements.* Chicago: Children's Press, 1982.

Vinke, Hermann. *The Short Life of Sophie Scholl.* New York: Harper & Row, 1984.

Vogel, Ilse-Margaret. *Bad Times, Good Friends.* New York: Harcourt Brace Javanovich, 1992.

Weinstein, Irving. *That Denmark Might Live; The Saga of Danish Resistance in World War II.* Philadelphia: Macrae Smith, 1967.

Zeinert, Karen. *The Warsaw Ghetto Uprising* Brookfield, CT.: Millbrook Press, 1993.

Secret Weapons, Spies, Sabotage:

Andryszewski, Tricia. *The Amazing Life of Moe Berg: Catcher, Scholar, Spy.* Brookfield, CT: Millbrook Press, 1996.

Daily, Robert. *The Code Talkers.* New York: Franklin Watts, 1995.

Goldstone, Robert C. *Sinister Touches; The Secret War Against Hitler.* New York: Dial Press, 1992.

Jones, Catherine. *Navajo Code Talkers; Native American Heroes.* Greensboro: Tudor Publications, 1997.

Halter, Jon C. *Top Secret Projects of World War II.* New York: J. Messner, 1978.

Lawson, Don. *The Secret World War II.* New York: Franklin Watts, 1978.

Marrin, Albert. *The Secret Armies.* New York: Atheneum, 1985.

Index

Italic numerals indicate volume numbers.

Illustrations are marked by (ill.).

Anzio *2:* 237-238
Appeasement *1:* 21-22
Arcadia Conference *2:* 208-209
Ardennes Forest *1:* 48-49, 49 (ill.)
   2: 292
Ardennes offensive (*see* Battle of
   the Bulge)
Area bombing *1:* 188-189, 193
Armia Krajowa (AK) (*see* Home
   Army [Polish])
Armistice
   French-German (1940) *1:* 54
   World War I *1:* 4
Army Group Center (German)
   1: 81-82, *2:* 279-280
Army Group North (German) *1:* 81
Arsenal of Democracy *1:* 63, 106
Asia, and the Pacific *2:* 307 (ill.)
Asia for the Asians policy *1:* 31,
   2: 414
Athens *1:* 75-76, 74 (ill.), 136
Atlantic Charter *2:* 208, 414
Atlantic Wall *2:* 254-255,
   255 (ill.), 353
Atlantic, Battle of (*see* Battle
   of the Atlantic)
Atomic bomb *2:* 223, 337-344,
   338 (ill.), 340 (ill.), 363-368
Atrocities *1:* 30, 32, 157-179,
   2: 218-219, 298-299,
Attu *2:* 316
Auschwitz *1:* 178-179, 178 (ill.)
   202, *2:* 297
Australia *1:* 61, 101-102,
   2: 312, 393
Australian troops *2:* 318-319
Austria *1:* 4, 21, 160, 162, *2:* 403
Axis *1:* 69, 72, 75 (ill.), 103,
   2: 205, 224-226
Axis Sally (Mildred Gillars) *2:* 372

B

B-25 bomber *1:* 101
B-29 bomber (superfortress)
   2: 327-328, 334-335
Babi Yar *1:* 171
Baby boom, *2:* 406
Badoglio, Marshal Pietro *2:* 235
Bagration, Operation *2:* 278- 282
Barbarossa, Operation *1:* 77-82,
   79 (ill.)
Bari, Italy *1:* 195

Bataan *1:* 96-97, *2:* 327
Bataan Death March *1:* 97
Battle of Britain *1:* 55-60, 58 (ill.),
   59 (ill.), 182 (ill.), 185-186,
   2: 201 (ill.), 360
Battle of Midway *1:* 102-103
Battle of the Atlantic *1:* 66-69,
   68 (ill.), *2:* 227
Battle of the Bulge *2:* 292 (ill.),
   292-294
   and African-American troops
   1: 115
   and intelligence *2:* 346
Battle of the Coral Sea *1:* 100
   (ill.), 101-102
BBC (*see* British Broadcasting
   Corporation)
Beethoven's Fifth Symphony
   2: 371
Belarus (*see* White Russia)
Belgium *1:* 47-48, 49 (ill.), 138,
   183, *2:* 270, 355, 396
Belorussia (*see* White Russia)
Belzec concentration camp *1:* 173
Bengal, famine in (1943) *2:* 412
Bergman, Ingrid *2:* 382, 382 (ill.)
Berlin *1:* 191, *2:* 395 (ill.), 397 (ill.)
Berlin, Battle of *2:* 301-304
Bethe, Hans *2:* 366
Bielsko *1:* 164
Blücher (German battleship) *1:* 47
Black Code (American attaché
   code) *2:* 357
Black market *1:* 110, 112, 136
Black shirts (Italy) *1:* 12
Blackout *1:* 187, 200
Bletchley Park (Ultra
   headquarters) *2:* 358
Blitz (*see* Battle of Britain)
Blitzkrieg *1:* 40-41
Bogart, Humphrey *2:* 382, 382 (ill.)
Bohemia *1:* 23
Bombardment air, D-Day *2:* 264
Bombardment, naval, D-Day
   2: 264
Bomber Command (Royal Air
   Force) *1:* 188-189, 193
"Bomber" Harris (*see* Harris,
   Sir Arthur)
Bond drives *1:* 108
Bonin Islands *2:* 326 (ill.)
Book burnings *2:* 373
Bosnia *1:* 154-155

under occupation *1:* 136
withdrawal of German troops
from *2:* 299
Greenland *1:* 66
Grossen-Wannsee Conference
(*see* Wannsee Conference)
Groves, Leslie *2:* 367 (ill.)
Grynszpan, Hershel *1:* 160
Guadalcanal *2:* 314 (ill.), 314-316
and Navajo code-talkers *2:* 358
Guadalcanal Diary 2: 385
Guam *1:* 95, *2:* 320
Guernica (Spain), bombing of
1: 21
Guerrilla warfare
in Ethiopia *1:* 69
in occupied Europe *1:*144-147,
149-152, 155-156
"Gustav Line" (Italy)
2: 233 (ill.), 236

H

Halsey, Admiral William *2:* 313
Hamburg *1:* 190-191, 191 (ill.)
Hanford, Washington *2:* 366
Harlem riot (August 1943) *1:* 118
Harris, Sir Arthur
1: 189, 189 (ill.)
Hawaii *1:* 89
Health and disease
in occupied Europe *1:* 137
Hedgerows (Normandy) *2:* 268,
269 (ill.)
Heisenberg, Werner *2:* 364
Hepburn, Katherine *2:* 378
Heydrich, Reinhard *1:* 141,
164-165, 165 (ill.), 172
Himmler, Heinrich *1:* 134, 172
Hindenburg, Paul von *1:* 13-14,
18
Hirohito (Emperor of Japan)
1: 25, *2:* 335-337, 339-340
Hiroshima *2:* 224, 337-338,
338 (ill.), 340
Hitchcock, Alfred *2:* 379
Hitler Youth *1:* 204, *2:* 304 (ill.)
Hitler Youth Division (Waffen SS)
1: 204
Hitler, Adolf *1:* 19 (ill.), 20 (ill.),
54, 54 (ill.), 73, 76, 133, 157,
2: 210, 240 (ill.), 245, 273,
349, 256, 273, 356

death of *2:* 303
plot to kill *2:* 287-290
relations with generals
2: 240-241
rise to power *1:* 10-18
Hitler-Stalin Pact
(*see* Nazi-Soviet Pact)
HMS *Prince of Wales 1:* 98
HMS *Repulse 1:* 98
Hollywood *2:* 378-379, 383
Holocaust *1:* 157-179, 158 (ill.),
163 (ill.) 167 (ill.), 169 (ill.),
175 (ill.), 178 (ill.)
and children *1:* 202
Home Army (Polish) *1:* 35,
2: 282-284
and Warsaw uprising (1944)
2: 282-286
Home front *1:* 105-129
Hong Kong *1:* 95
Honolulu *1:* 89
Honshu *2:* 332
Hornet *1:* 103
Hostages *1:* 140-142
France *1:* 142
Greece *1:* 142
Hungarian army *1:* 78
Hungary *2:* 225
and communism *2:* 220
and Yugoslavia *1:* 74
army in Soviet Union *2:* 244
attack by Romania on *2:* 298
deaths in *2:* 393
German economic policy in
1: 135
Hunger winter (Netherlands)
1: 136
Hyper-inflation *1:* 8

I

Iceland *1:* 66
Ie Shima *2:* 388
Ikoku, Iva Toguri (TokyoRose)
2: 373
The Immortal Sergeant 2: 385
Imperialism *1:* 27
Incendiary bombs *1:* 188
India *1:* 61, 62 (ill.), 99
and Atlantic Charter *2:* 208
Bengal famine (1943) *2:* 412
independence movement in
2: 415 (ill.), 416
losses in the war *2:* 393

J